ZILLI'S ITALIAN FOOD FOR FRIENDS

ZILLI'S ITALIAN FOOD FOR FRIENDS

MOUTHWATERING RECIPES MADE FAST AND SIMPLE

ALDO ZILLI

metro

Published by Metro Publishing Ltd,
3 Bramber Court, 2 Bramber Road,
London W14 9PB, England

ISBN 1 84358 010 1

British Library Cataloguing-in-Publication Data: A catalogue record
for this book is available from the British Library.

Edited by Norma MacMillan
Designed by Roger Walker
Jacket design by ENVY
Food photography by Gus Filgate
Food stylist Susie Theodorou
Many thanks to Contemporary Ceramics for the loan of the following items used
in our photographs: coffee cup and saucer, and bowl by Hilary Roberts; and a
bowl by Karen Downing. Available from Contemporary Ceramics (020 7437 7605).
Typeset by SX Composing DTP, Rayleigh, Essex

Printed and bound in Italy by Eurolitho S.p.A, Milan

1 3 5 7 9 10 8 6 4 2

Papers used by Metro Publishing Ltd are natural, recyclable products made
from wood grown in sustainable forests. The manufacturing processes conform
to the environmental regulations of the country of origin.

Contents

Acknowledgements

Firstly, I would like to thank my family – my wife Jan and daughter Laura – for being so understanding whilst I was engrossed in this book. It involved many late nights and weekends at the office writing, and in the kitchen tasting, so I'm sure they will be pleased to have their husband and father back.

I would also like to thank Sarah Lewis for giving up her social life for this project. She worked wonders with my scrawl, organised all the liaison for the book and my life, and still managed to keep smiling. I think it's been a great learning experience for her, and hopefully this book will inspire her to get into the kitchen and cook ... one day!

I am extremely lucky to have had such a talented team around me, all very gifted in their own individual areas. Writing the recipes and cooking the food for the photographs turned out to be much more fun than I could have possibly imagined.

I would like say a big thank you to my chefs, Ron Irvine and Andy Campbell. Ron, my head chef at Zilli Fish restaurant, has been a great help. Whilst running Zilli Fish he still managed to find time to help me, which was greatly appreciated. Andy has been a great source of inspiration. He has worked extensively in Italy, and has an ability to be creative with food, approaching things in an innovative and unique way.

I would also like to thank my food stylist and home economist, Susie Theodorou. She worked wonders with my recipes and, knowing me as well as she does, was able to translate my ideas perfectly on to the plate. She also kept me, and everybody else, laughing throughout the whole process.

Many thanks to all my other chefs, managers and staff for doing such a good job without me; Gus Filgate for taking some truly wonderful pictures; my publishers, Metro Books; my agents, Limelight; Antonio Alfano from Ciborio; and Gabriele from Camisa deli.

A special thank you to my friends Bruce Burgess, Mandy Hawes, Stacey Young and Trevor Beattie, pictured (left to right) on the back cover, for agreeing to be part of this book.

ALDO ZILLI

Introduction

To those who know me well, the title of this book should mean everything. To those of you who do not know me, it will soon become apparent that I just love being with people and looking after them. This book is for people who, like me, take great pleasure in entertaining and cooking for friends.

Zilli's Italian Food for Friends is a collection of recipes that I have enjoyed cooking over the years, either in my restaurants or at home for friends and family. My main aim is to give you an insight into Italian cooking, showing you how easy it is to create delicious dishes. Forget the fuss! Simplicity is the key. All of my recipes are achievable by the cook at home, even a novice cook. My recipes can be used for dinner parties or celebrations, or just for simple suppers. Some of them are so quick and easy that they are great for working people who do not have much time to cook.

Although I love cooking all types of food, my favourite has to be pasta. I adore both cooking and eating pasta – it is a great energy food as well as being enormously versatile. Pasta is definitely the most popular food in all my restaurants. It has been great to see the increasing popularity of Italian food over the past few years, to such an extent that it is now the most popular cuisine in the UK. Most of the ingredients used in Italian cooking are now readily available in supermarkets. If you keep your storecupboard well stocked, you will always be always prepared, whatever the occasion. (I've made some suggestions in my Italian Ingredients section on pages 1–8.)

When I started work on this book, I began by remembering who had influenced me the most and inspired me to start cooking. Undoubtedly the biggest single influence has to be my mother. As the youngest in the family, I was often kept in the kitchen with my mother and gradually, over the years, I picked up her ability to cook. Many of the recipes I use now are based on dishes she used to cook when I was a child. She inspired me to go into catering when I realised that it was something I really enjoyed doing.

Writing this book has been a huge commitment, requiring a good deal of time. However, it has been one of the most challenging and fulfiling tasks I have ever undertaken. I hope my recipes inspire you to get into the kitchen. Cooking truly is fun – it should never be regarded as a chore. Be adventurous and experiment, adapting recipes to suit your personal taste. If they do not always work out the first time, just try again. Have patience, keep your sense of humour and enjoy yourself.

Buon appetito!

Aldo's Italian Ingredients

Storecupboard staples

Anchovies

Anchovies are used on pizzas, in *antipasti* and salads and to season sauces as they melt very easily. In all good supermarkets, you will find canned anchovy fillets packed in olive oil and whole anchovies packed in salt, as well as anchovy paste in tubes. All of these different anchovies can be used in the same way, so you can take your pick or stock all three. If using salted ones, thoroughly rinse and bone them before using.

Balsamic Vinegar

This delicious mahogany-coloured vinegar is aged in wooden barrels over many years, with the type of wood and the size of the barrel changing each year. This process gives the vinegar its sweet smell and exquisite subtle flavour. Balsamic vinegar is used primarily uncooked, in dressings, for example, and you might like to try sprinkling it on cheese or fruit. I would recommend that you invest in a vintage bottle of balsamic vinegar, at least 8 years old – it is expensive, but you will really notice the difference in flavour between it and younger balsamic vinegars.

Beans

Borlotti and cannellini beans are the ones I tend to use most. They are available dried and in cans. Although canned beans are quick and convenient to use, and fine for casseroles and soups, I would recommend that you cook your own dried beans for salads because they will have a better texture. Dried beans should be soaked overnight, then covered with fresh cold water, bought up to the boil and boiled for at least 10 minutes. (This ensures the enzymes in the beans will not produce toxins.) After the initial boiling, skim the froth from the surface, reduce the heat so the water is simmering and continue cooking until the beans are tender (1–2 hours).

Biscuits

Amaretti are little almond-flavoured biscuits, crisp and very light. They are often sold wrapped in pairs in pastel-coloured papers. Amaretti can be used in desserts, or served with coffee or Vin Santo.

Savoiardi are sponge finger biscuits, firmer and drier than English sponge fingers. They are used to make desserts such as *tiramisù*.

Capers

Capers are the small flower buds from a Sicilian bush that grows near the coast. The flower buds are preserved by being packed in salt or pickled in vinegar. I think the small capers from Sicily are the best ones. Capers are used to flavour fish dishes, as well as being added to *antipasti* and salads.

Dried wild mushrooms

A very precious ingredient, dried porcini, or ceps, and other wild mushrooms can be used in small quantity to give a great depth of flavour to a dish. If a recipe calls for fresh porcini and you cannot obtain any (or they are too expensive), you can substitute a small quantity of dried porcini plus fresh cultivated mushrooms such as chestnut or open cap. Before using dried mushrooms they need to be soaked in a bowl of hot water for 15–20 minutes, to rehydrate them. The soaking liquid, which will have a wonderful flavour, can be used as part of the cooking liquid in the dish, but take care to discard the sediment at the bottom of the bowl, which will be dirt and grit from the mushrooms.

Flour

You can buy lots of different types of flour, but only a few are essential for your storecupboard. I would always keep white bread flour, plain flour and cornflour, which will cover all your basic needs for bread-making, pastries, desserts and thickening stocks and sauces. If you want to make pasta dough, I would recommend that you also have some Italian type 00 flour (available in delis and many supermarkets). To be sure that flour does not become damp from the humidity in the kitchen, remove it from the packet and store it in a tightly closed glass jar.

Marinated Vegetables

Jars of marinated vegetables, simply packed in oil or with added flavourings, are well worth keeping in your storecupboard. When you are entertaining you can simply toast some ciabatta bread and then serve it with any of the marinated vegetables that you have on hand. If you have time it is very easy to prepare your own: roast or grill the vegetables, cover with olive oil, season and leave for a day before using.

Olive Oil

In the past few years olive oil has become one of the most widely used ingredients in the British kitchen. I use olive oil in most of my recipes, choosing the type according to the dish I am making. The best olive oil is unrefined virgin oil, which is separated into two grades, 'extra virgin' and 'virgin', according to its acidity. I would never use extra virgin olive oil for shallow or deep frying or searing – virgin olive oil is fine for these – but would recommend it for making dressings and cold sauces such as pesto.

There are a multitude of different olive oils from various regions across Italy, so here are a few tips for you.
Umbria: produces much stronger olive oil than other regions.
Liguria: makes much lighter olive oils.
Puglia: most commercial and so produces the cheapest oils.
Tuscany: makes the best oil, in my opinion. I would recommend that you invest in a good bottle of Tuscan olive oil.

Olive oil can be flavoured by simply adding herbs, chilli or lemon. Leave for at least 3 weeks before using, except for lemon which only takes 2 or 3 days to flavour the oil.

Olives

Green olives are harvested before they are ripe, whereas black ones are left until they are over-ripe, which gives them a stronger flavour. There is an endless choice of olives available now, from small to large, pitted or with stone in, flavoured or plain. My two favourite olives are the large green ones and those stuffed with almonds. With the stone-in variety, try bruising them slightly and then marinating in an olive oil, garlic and balsamic vinegar dressing.

A good mail order source for olives is Fresh Olives Direct (Unit 1, Hanover Industrial Estate, Acton Lane, London NW10 7NB; tel 020 8453 1918/fax 020 8838 1913). They sell many different kinds of olives, as well as other Mediterranean delicacies such as tapenade, sun-dried red peppers and tomatoes, balsamic vinegar, and a range of olive oils and flavoured oils. Call them for a catalogue.

Panettone

This very light sweet bread has a texture rather like a dry sponge cake. It contains raisins, pine nuts and candied citron, and is baked in a tall cylindrical mould. It is delicious served plain or buttered with coffee or can be used in desserts.

Pasta

Pasta is the perfect base for a quick meal for the unexpected visitor or hungry children, so always keep a good selection of dried pastas in your storecupboard – opting for brand names rather than supermarket own brands. You might also want to store some fresh pasta in the freezer; it can be cooked from frozen. I would recommend that you stick to plain, not coloured, fresh pasta as you can never be sure what has been used to colour it. If you want to have spinach pasta, for example, make it yourself (see page 214).

Pine nuts or kernels

These are little creamy-white seeds, long and thin, taken from the cones of pine trees. Pine nuts have a very delicate flavour and aroma, making them perfect for use in desserts as well as in savoury dishes and sauces such as pesto. As pine nuts can go rancid quite quickly, don't keep them too long. To toast pine nuts (and other nuts such as walnuts and flaked almonds), put them in a dry frying pan and shake and stir constantly over a moderate heat for 3–4 minutes until golden brown.

Polenta flour

This yellow maize flour is used mainly to make wet or set polenta (see page 217), to be served as an accompaniment or like bread, but can also be the thickener for sauces, soups, stews and so on, and the basis for sweet puddings and cakes.

Rice

I would recommend having two types of rice in the storecupboard. For making risotto, keep a special risotto rice such as Arborio – its plump medium-long grains can absorb liquid without becoming too soft. Risotto rice is also good for puddings. Basmati rice, with its long grains, is the one to use for pilafs and stuffings.

Saffron

Taken from the crocus flower, saffron has a unique aroma and the ability to give food a beautiful yellow colour. In Italy it is most commonly used in risottos and fish soups. I suggest you use saffron thread rather than powdered saffron as the latter tends to be less fresh and pungent.

Salt

Refined flaked sea salt is an essential for the storecupboard. When using salt in cooking, it is important to add it at the right moment. For example, steaks should be salted at the last minute, not at the beginning of grilling or frying, and roasts should be salted once they gain colour (salt draws moisture out, and this moisture would prevent the meat from browning and searing). For pasta, salt should be added to the water once it starts boiling (salt raises the boiling point of water, so it would take longer for the water to come to the boil). A good tip is to add some salt to the water when boiling eggs as this will prevent the shells from cracking.

Stock cubes

Cubes are a quick alternative to fresh stock, whether bought or home-made, so are useful to have on hand. Stock from a cube can be used in risottos, soups and sauces.

Tomatoes and tomato sauce

Where would Italian cooking be without tomatoes and tomato sauce? I use a lot of tomatoes in my cooking – fresh when in season or chopped, peeled tomatoes in cans at other times of the year. Canned tomatoes are essential in the storecupboard. I always make my own tomato sauce, and recommend that you do too. You will notice that the taste is quite different from bought tomato sauce – so much better! Use plenty of herbs and olive oil to finish the sauce off.

Tuna

Buy good-quality canned tuna packed in oil. It's so useful for salads and pasta dishes. *Bresaola di tonno*, which is an air-dried tuna from Sardinia, is a real delicacy. You can find it at good Italian delis or by mail order from Vallebona Sardinian Gourmet (Tel; 020 8944 5665). I serve it sliced into very thin strips with rocket, Parmesan, lemon and extra virgin oil.

Fresh ingredients

Bitter leaves

These include dandelion, rocket, radicchio, Treviso chicory, curly endive or frisée and escarole. All of these have been popular in Italy for some time, and I love their flavours. They grew wild on my father's farm, and my mother used to make a fantastic salad with them called 'Misticanza'. If you find these leaves too bitter, try dressing them with well-aged balsamic vinegar – the sweet flavour it gives will be a revelation.

Cheeses

- Fontina is a semi-soft cow's milk cheese that has a delicate, nutty, almost honey flavour to it. It is used extensively in northern Italy for cooking.
- Gorgonzola takes its name from a small town not far from Milan. This full-fat, blue-veined cheese was initially called Stracchino di Gorgonzola, from *stracco*, meaning tired, as it was made from the milk of tired cows.
- Mascarpone is a typical cream cheese from Lombardy. It is not so much a cheese as a mild

delicate cream, the colour of which ranges from snow white to straw. Mascarpone is used in a variety of desserts and pasta sauces.

- Mozzarella comes in many different shapes – 125g (5oz) globes, cubes, blocks, cherry-sized balls and small morsels. Most of the mozzarella in supermarkets is made from fresh cow's milk. The delicious buffalo mozzarella (*mozzarella di bufala*) is made from 100 per cent pure buffalo's milk. It is porcelain white and springy in texture, with a characteristic milky flavour and aftertaste. Pear-shaped smoked mozzarella is also available.
- Parmesan is hard semi-fat cheese with a smooth golden rind. It fractures into large flakes when cut. True Parmesan, or Parmigiano Reggiano, has a registered trade mark, guaranteed by the Parmigiano Reggiano Cheese Consortium, which shows that it is made exclusively in the traditional area comprising the territories of Parma, Reggio, Emilia, Modena and Bologna. The method of making and ripening this cheese has remained unchanged for 7 centuries.
- Pecorino, a ewe's milk cheese, is made throughout central and southern Italy. The best-known varieties are toscano, romano, siciliano and sardo (from Sardinia). Pecorino can vary in flavour depending on where it has been produced and the amount of time it has been aged.
- Ricotta is a fresh cheese made in the same style as English cottage cheese. Traditionally made from the whey of ewe's milk, it is now largely made from that of cows or, sometimes, buffalo milk. Light and delicate in flavour, ricotta is used in many desserts, as a pasta filling and in soups or eaten on its own.

Chillies

Fresh chillies can be found all year round at good supermarkets. I prefer red chillies for cooking, but either green or red can be used to flavour olive oil.

Courgette blossoms

These are the bright orange-yellow flowers from courgettes and other squashes. The flowers are very soft in texture and perishable. They can be stuffed with cheese, vegetables or shellfish and then deep-fried in batter or baked.

Garlic

Garlic is used all over the world, but plays a particularly important part in Italian cooking. For a mild garlic flavour in a dish, peel the clove and just crush it slightly (the more you chop or crush garlic – particularly in a garlic press – the stronger the flavour will be). Unfortunately, the smell of garlic on the breath is thought to be slightly unsociable. To eliminate the aftertaste, slice the clove in half and remove the central core before crushing or chopping. Or you might try chewing parsley.

Herbs

- Basil can easily be grown in gardens or window boxes (always try to buy small plants and water them regularly), so you can have a fresh supply throughout the spring and summer. This herb is the main ingredient in a traditional pesto sauce, and is delicious in tomato dishes. Tear the delicate basil leaves with your fingers rather than chopping them.
- Marjoram is used mainly in northern Italy, in the Liguria region. It is a very good flavouring for soups and sauces, although cooking will destroy much of its delicate flavour.
- Oregano is a very common herb in Italian cooking. Dried oregano is fine for pizzas, but for grilled meats, tomatoes and salad dressings, always use fresh oregano.
- Sage is widely used in Italian cooking, particularly when roasting meat and for flavouring butter. It is easy to grow.

Deep-fried herb leaves make an attractive and delicious garnish. First wash the leaves and pat them completely dry, then deep fry for 1–2 minutes until bright green and crisp. Drain on kitchen paper.

Italian sausages

Unlike many English sausages, Italian sausages are made only with meat – no water or breadcrumbs are added. I recommend that you buy sausages from a good Italian deli. My favourite sausages, which originate from my home village, are marinated in red wine with herbs and then dried for 2 weeks.

Mortadella

A large, round, pure pork sausage with a smooth texture, this is often studded with pistachio nuts and may be flavoured with white wine and coriander. It is sold ready to eat.

Pancetta

This is Italian streaky bacon. It may be smoked or green (unsmoked) and flavoured with dried herbs or spices. It has a slightly sweet taste and a low water content, which means that it retains its shape and flavour when cooked. Diced or cut into matchstick-size pieces, it is widely used in pasta sauces as well as stews and casseroles. It can also be cut into thin slices to wrap around game or other meat to prevent it from becoming too dry.

Shallots

This small bulb is related to onions and garlic, but is much more delicate in flavour and aroma.

Squid ink

Called *nero di seppia* in Italian, this is used for colouring food such as risotto and pasta. It has a very distinctive flavour. If you don't have time to clean fresh squid and remove the ink sac, you can buy the ink in sachets from a good fishmonger.

Zampone

These boned pig's trotters, stuffed with a delicious pork and wine sausage called cotechino, are usually bought precooked, in which case they only need to be heated through.

Notes

Eggs

In all recipes, medium eggs should be used unless otherwise stated.

Some recipes use raw or undercooked eggs. Because of the risk of salmonella poisoning, these recipes should be avoided by the elderly, young children, pregnant women and people whose immunity has been compromised by illness.

Beef and beef offal

I have included recipes for beef and beef offal in this book. In view of the recent concerns about the safety of beef, I have, where appropriate, suggested alternatives, but sometimes there just is no alternative. In those cases, you may want to try organic beef which is believed to be BSE free. For information about organic meat (and other produce) and where to buy it, contact The Soil Association, Bristol House, 40-56 Victoria Street, Bristol BS1 6BY (tel 0117 929 0661/fax 0117 925 2504). They publish a booklet called *The Organic Directory* (available on their website www.soilassociation.org).

Aldo's Italian Wine Cellar

Wines from Abruzzo

The people of Abruzzo love their vigorous wines, and consider it appropriate to indulge on just about any occasion. Montepulciano is the main grape grown in the Abruzzo region. It produces what I consider to be the best red wine, Montepulciano d'Abruzzo. This can often be mistaken for the Tuscan Vino Nobile di Montepulciano, which is another very good dry red wine. I am also very fond of the dry red Marsicano. Montepulciano d'Abruzzo, popular because of its depth of taste, aroma and colour, is good with both meat and game.

Cerasuolo d'Abruzzo is a dry soft rosé made from Montepulciano grapes that have been fermented without the skins. Rosé wine is excellent served chilled with spicy food as it will not overpower the dish – it quenches your thirst while at the same time it cleanses your palate. I would recommend this rosé with Tagliata alla Diavola (see page 149), which is steak with a garlic and chilli sauce.

Trebbiano d'Abruzzo, also known as Abruzzo Bianco, is a dry white wine with a fresh delicate bouquet and a characteristic straw yellow colour. It is excellent served with fish such as bass. You'll find this wine in Italian delis and in supermarkets with a good wine selection.

Other local wines include Biferno, available in red, white and rosé, and Pentro di Isernia, both red and white, which are produced in Molise.

Wines from other regions of Italy

A red wine that I always keep at home in my cellar, ready for entertaining friends, is Barolo from Piemonte. This full-bodied, long-lived wine is good with roasts, game such as venison and strong cheeses such as Gorgonzola. Other wines from this region include the well-known Asti Spumante and Dolcetto, both of which are very good with desserts or as an aperitif.

I am also very fond of wines from the north-east. On a recent visit to Milan, I enjoyed a white wine called Lugana. Served chilled, it goes very well with fried fish such as Calamari Delicati (see page 13). Soave, which is a refreshing and light white wine from Verona, is a good partner for turkey and chicken dishes such as Tacchino Canzanese (see page 73) or Suprema di Pollo Ripieno (see page 71). One of the red wines from Lombardy that I would recommend is Sassella, which is often served with pig's trotters. The famous red Valpolicella from Lake Garda is normally drunk with risottos such as Risotto Vecchia Romagna (see page 38), made with chicken, Parma ham and brandy.

Emilia-Romagna is the home of Parmigiano, balsamic vinegar and lambrusco wines. Lambrusco wines are surprisingly underrated – I would certainly recommend the more expensive dry varieties (not the screw tops!). Served chilled, they are perfect for barbecues, and go well with chicken dishes such as Galletto al Forno (see page 74), as well as the popular Italian starter, Antipasti Misti (see page 188).

The last time I visited Tuscany I ate in a very impressive restaurant where the food was fantastic. We started with the region's traditional white bean soup (see my recipe for Ribollita on page 121), served with lots of crusty bread and extra virgin olive oil, and indulged in a beautiful red wine, Rosso di Montalcino.

Orvieto, one of my favourite towns in Umbria, gives its name to one of the region's white wines, Orvieto Abboccato, which was always very popular in my first restaurant. It is good with pasta dishes such as Fettuccine al Salmone e Tartufo (see page 22).

When in Rome, or eating Roman dishes, I suggest you do what the Romans do – drink local wines. Rome is situated in the region of Lazio and is one of Italy's most productive wine areas. Try their range of Frascatis or the rather strangely named Est! Est! Est! from Montefiascone, which is a straw-yellow muscat wine.

In this country Marsala is only known as a cooking wine, but in its native Sicily it is regarded as a liqueur wine. It is often used in desserts, most notably Zabaione (see page 86). I would suggest investing in a good bottle of Marsala as it makes a perfect drink at Christmas time – why not try it with Panettone ai Mirtilli (see page 194)?

Centerbe, whose name means 'one hundred herbs', is a very powerful 70 per cent proof liqueur. It has a unique flavour, and is considered to be a good remedy for colds and other illnesses. Aurum is another excellent liqueur, produced in the fishing town of Pescara. You will see that I have used Vin Santo, or holy wine, in one of my recipes. This sweet smelling liqueur makes a delightful aperitif or can be the conclusion to a meal.

Spring/Summer

Calamari Delicati
Deep-fried calamari

These make very good party nibbles as well as a starter. Or serve them with a salad for a main course. My daughter Laura's favourite is with French fries and mayonnaise for dipping.

Serves 4
Preparation time: 10 minutes
Cooking time: 10 minutes

150ml (5fl oz) single cream
3 egg yolks
30ml (2 tablespoons) freshly grated Parmesan cheese
30ml (2 tablespoons) plain flour
1 garlic clove, peeled and crushed
5ml (1 teaspoon) dried oregano
salt and freshly ground black pepper
oil for deep-frying
6 squid, cleaned and bodies cut into rings

- Pour the cream into a large bowl and beat in the egg yolks, cheese, flour, garlic and oregano to make a smooth batter. Season with freshly ground black pepper.
- Heat enough oil in a deep pan for deep-frying. When hot enough the oil should be 160–180°C, 325–350°F; a piece of bread dropped into the oil will sizzle and become golden brown in 30 seconds.
- Dip the squid rings and tentacles into the batter, one at a time, and put into the oil. Fry for 2–3 minutes until golden brown. Drain on kitchen paper and serve immediately, sprinkled with salt.

Gratin di Verdure
Vegetable gratin

In the summer you can serve this for a barbecue, plain or sprinkled with balsamic vinegar.

Serves 4
Preparation time: 5 minutes
Cooking time: 8–12 minutes

800g (1¾lb) baby vegetables, such as courgettes, carrots, asparagus, spring onions and mange
   tout, trimmed or peeled where necessary
6 eggs
150ml (5fl oz) single cream
salt and freshly ground black pepper
100g (4oz) butter, cubed
60ml (4 tablespoons) chopped fresh flat-leaf pasrley
60ml (4 tablespoons) dried breadcrumbs
60ml (4 tablespoons) freshly grated Parmesan cheese

- Thinly slice all the vegetables into strips. Place in the top of a steamer, or in a colander set over a pan of boiling salted water, and steam for 5–8 minutes until just tender yet still crisp.
- Meanwhile, place the eggs in a bowl and beat in the cream. Season with salt and freshly ground black pepper. Heat a little of the butter in a non-stick pan over a low heat and cook the eggs for 3 minutes until softly scrambled. Stir in three-quarters of the parsley.
- Pre-heat the grill to medium-hot. Divide the eggs among 4 small gratin dishes and top with the steamed vegetables. Mix the breadcrumbs with the Parmesan and sprinkle over the vegetables. Dot with the remaining butter. Grill for 3–4 minutes until golden.
- Sprinkle with the remaining parsley and serve immediately.

Cervo al Finocchio Selvatico
Venison fillet with fennel and Parmesan

This is my favourite dressing, but you can alter the ingredients according to your personal taste. For example, you may want to add some strong mustard or goat's cheese.

Serves 4
Preparation time: 10 minutes
Cooking time: 5 minutes

60ml (4 tablespoons) olive oil
juice of 1 lemon
15ml (1 tablespoon) flaked sea salt
30ml (2 tablespoons) freshly ground black pepper
450g (1lb) lean venison fillet
4 heads wild fennel or 1–2 fennel bulbs, trimmed and thinly sliced
100g (4oz) fresh Parmesan shavings

- Mix together the oil, lemon juice, salt and pepper. Rub the venison with this dressing on all sides. Reserve the remaining dressing.
- Heat a griddle until almost smoking. Put the venison fillet on the pan and grill for 5 minutes, turning once. Remove and leave to cool.
- With a sharp knife, finely slice the meat and arrange on a large platter or individual plates.
- Cover the venison with the fennel slices and Parmesan shavings. Add a touch of the remaining oil and lemon dressing and serve.

Cape Sante al Rosmarino
Skewers of scallops with rosemary sprigs

Ideally use large king scallops as they have more flavour than smaller ones (if using smaller scallops, double the quantity). I cooked this for Tiffany Dark from the Telegraph at a barbecue for the newspaper, and she loved it so much she has since visited Zilli Fish to indulge in this dish again.

Serves 4
Preparation time: 15 minutes
Cooking time: 10 minutes

8 king scallops
8 long stalks of fresh rosemary, leaves removed
juice of 1 lemon
75ml (5 tablespoons) extra virgin olive oil
15ml (1 tablespoon) flaked sea salt
50g (2oz) plain flour
salt and freshly ground black pepper
1 medium onion, peeled and thinly sliced into rings
vegetable oil for deep-frying

- Thread each scallop on to a rosemary stalk. Mix the lemon juice and 45ml (3 tablespoons) of the olive oil in a bowl and season with some of the salt flakes. Place the scallops in the lemon juice mixture and leave to marinate for 10 minutes.
- Meanwhile, place the flour in a bowl and season with salt and freshly ground black pepper. Add the onion rings to the flour and toss to coat all over. Heat enough vegetable oil in a deep pan for deep-frying until a piece of onion dropped into the oil sizzles immediately. Add the onion rings to the hot oil, in 2 batches, and deep-fry for 2–3 minutes until crisp and golden. Drain on kitchen paper.
- Pre-heat the grill to medium-hot. Place the scallops on a foil-lined grill pan. Grill for 4 minutes on each side until golden brown and tender.
- Arrange the scallops on one large or 4 individual serving plates with the onions. Drizzle with the remaining olive oil and sprinkle with the rest of the salt flakes to serve.

Focaccia Ripiena
Focaccia stuffed with mozzarella and mortadella

Mortadella reminds me of my childhood. Being inexpensive, it was always on our dinner table. It is now very easy to get in this country, in delis and supermarkets.

Serves 8
Preparation time: 10 minutes
Cooking time: 15 minutes

30ml (2 tablespoons) olive oil
1 large Spanish onion, peeled and thinly sliced
1 quantity baked focaccia (see page 216)
2 x 125g (5oz) mozzarella cheeses, sliced
4 slices of mortadella
4 plum tomatoes, sliced

- Pre-heat the oven to 200°C, 400°F, Gas Mark 6. Heat the oil in a frying pan, add the onion and cook for 5 minutes until soft and just beginning to brown.
- Slice the focaccia in half horizontally and open it up like a book. Arrange the mozzarella and mortadella slices on the bottom half and close the focaccia. Sprinkle the top with the onions and sliced tomatoes.
- Bake for 10 minutes until the cheese is melting and the onions are golden brown. Cut into squares and serve immediately.

Reginette all'Anatra
Reginette pasta with duck sauce

Reginette pasta is the curlier version of the thick-ribboned pappardelle pasta (which can also be used). I discovered this recipe when I was 16 whilst working in a small hotel in my home village. It was my first job, and I'd been sent there by my father to work as a comi porter. It was extremely hard work, but taught me a lot at a very young age. A good red wine is required for this pasta dish. In my family, we used to drink home-made wine, but as this is not available to everyone I suggest Cabernet Sauvignon Trentino Rigiou. It's a deep red with wonderful aromas and flavours of ripe red fruits.

Serves 4
Preparation time: 20 minutes
Cooking time: 30 minutes

350g (12oz) reginette or pappardelle pasta (see page 214 for home-made pappardelle)
60ml (4 tablespoons) freshly grated pecorino cheese

For the duck sauce
2 x 200g (7oz) duck breasts
75ml (5 tablespoons) olive oil
1 bunch of spring onions, trimmed and finely chopped
2 carrots, peeled and finely chopped
1 celery stick, trimmed and finely chopped
1 garlic clove, peeled and crushed
1 sprig of fresh thyme
2 bay leaves
salt and freshly ground black pepper
2 beef tomatoes, skinned, seeded and finely diced
1 fresh red chilli, seeded and finely chopped
1 small bunch of fresh basil, stalks discarded and leaves shredded

- To make the duck sauce, finely slice the duck breast. Heat 15ml (1 tablespoon) of the oil in a frying pan and add the duck; fry for 5 minutes until golden brown all over. Drain on kitchen paper.
- In a saucepan, heat 15ml (1 tablespoon) of the oil and add the spring onions, carrots, celery, garlic, thyme and bay leaves. Season well with salt and freshly ground black pepper. Cover and cook (sweat) for 10 minutes, stirring occasionally. Add the diced tomatoes and strips of duck to the sauce with the remaining oil, the chilli and basil. Simmer for a further 5 minutes.

- Meanwhile, cook the pasta in a large pan of boiling salted water for 5–8 minutes, or according to the instructions on the packet, until *al dente*. Drain and mix with the sauce and cheese. Serve immediately.

Spaghetti alla Crudaiola
Spaghetti with sun-dried tomatoes and fresh tomato cream sauce

If possible, use dry sun-dried tomatoes and not those preserved in olive oil because they will give a better flavour to the dish. (If you only have tomatoes packed in oil, rinse them to remove excess oil.) You could also add other Mediterranean vegetables such as sun-dried aubergines and peppers. Kathy Lloyd loves this dish – I've cooked it for her on many occasions – and it is also particularly popular with children.

Serves 6
Preparation time: 20 minutes
Cooking time: 15–20 minutes

400g (14oz) spaghetti

For the tomato sauce
450g (1lb) tomatoes ripened on the vine
6 sun-dried tomatoes
45ml (3 tablespoons) olive oil
1 onion, peeled and finely chopped
1 garlic clove, peeled and crushed
300ml (10fl oz) single cream
1 bunch of fresh basil, stalks discarded and leaves shredded
salt and freshly ground black pepper

- Remove the tomatoes from the vine and place in a bowl. Cover with boiling water and leave for 1 minute, then drain and peel off the skins. Halve the tomatoes and discard the seeds; roughly chop the flesh.
- Place the dry sun-dried tomatoes in a pan of boiling water and boil for 5 minutes. Drain and thinly slice the tomatoes.
- Cook the spaghetti in a large pan of boiling salted water for 6–8 minutes, or according to the instructions on the packet, until *al dente*.
- Meanwhile, heat the oil in a large pan and fry the onion and garlic for 3–5 minutes until golden brown. Add the sun-dried tomatoes, fresh tomatoes, cream, basil and freshly ground black pepper to taste. Remove the sauce from the heat.
- Drain the spaghetti and quickly add to the sauce, tossing to mix. Adjust the seasoning if necessary. Serve immediately, with more freshly ground black pepper.

Trenette al Pesto
Trenette with mixed herb pesto sauce

Pesto is a great condiment for pasta, particularly the flat spaghetti called trenette, as well as for gnocchi and fish. For the best results, add the pesto to the pasta away from the heat and don't reheat. There is quite a difference between home-made and bought pesto, as you will see when you try this mixed herb version or the basil one on page 208.

Serves 4
Preparation time: 20 minutes
Cooking time: 10 minutes

350g (12oz) trenette pasta

For the pesto sauce
2 sprigs of fresh flat-leaf parsley
2 bunches of fresh basil
30ml (2 tablespoons) pine nuts
3 garlic cloves, peeled and crushed
50g (2oz) Parmesan cheese, freshly grated
150ml (5fl oz) olive oil
salt and freshly ground black pepper

- To make the pesto sauce, use either a pestle and mortar or a food processor. Pound or blend the herbs together, then add the pine nuts and garlic followed by the Parmesan cheese, pounding or blending to mix. Gradually add the olive oil, blending well between each addition.
- Cook the pasta in a large pan of boiling salted water for 10 minutes, or according to the instructions on the packet, until *al dente*. Drain, reserving 50ml (2fl oz) of the cooking liquid.
- Turn the pasta into a warm bowl and mix in the pesto sauce, adding enough of the reserved cooking liquid to thin the pesto a little so it coats the pasta. Adjust the seasoning and serve immediately.

Pasta

Fettuccine al Salmone e Tartufo
Fettuccine with smoked salmon, leeks and truffle oil

Truffle oil is now available in all Italian delis. However, I would advise you to invest in one small truffle in the autumn when truffles are in season. Then you can flavour your own oils as well as grating a little onto pasta. You may have to take out a second mortgage to afford a truffle, but the flavour is so wonderful that it's worth it! This recipe is a favourite of Richard Parks, Group Director of Programmes at Capital Radio, who is a close friend and good customer.

Serves 4
Preparation time: 20 minutes
Cooking time: 20 minutes

350g (12oz) fettuccine (see page 214 for home-made fettuccine)

For the sauce
100g (4oz) butter
1 large leek, trimmed and finely chopped
225g (8oz) smoked salmon, cut into strips
300ml (10fl oz) Salsa Besciamella (see page 206)
2.5ml (½ teaspoon) freshly grated nutmeg
salt and freshly ground black pepper
300ml (10fl oz) double cream
5ml (1 teaspoon) white truffle oil

- To make the sauce, melt the butter in a large frying pan, add the leek and stir well. Fry for 5 minutes until golden. Add the salmon, then stir in the béchamel sauce. Cook for 5 minutes.
- Meanwhile, cook the fettuccine in a large pan of boiling salted water for 5 minutes, or according to the instructions on the packet, until *al dente*. Drain.
- Season the sauce with the nutmeg and salt and freshly ground black pepper to taste, then stir in the drained pasta. Gradually stir in the cream and truffle oil. Serve immediately.

Linguine alle Cape Sante e Vongole
Linguine pasta with scallops, clams and leeks

For this dish go to a good fishmonger who will make sure you get fresh clams and cleaned scallops. If preparing the shellfish yourself, soak the clams for 30 minutes in cold salted water. Open the scallop shells with a small pointed knife, remove the scallops and trim them. This is fantastic on a hot summer's day, served with a tasty salad and plenty of focaccia bread to mop up the juices. Anneka Rice loves this dish – I've often cooked it for her when she has visited my restaurant.

Serves 4
Preparation time: 20 minutes
Cooking time: 20 minutes

350g (12oz) fresh linguine pasta
2 fresh basil leaves, shredded
60ml (4 tablespoons) chopped fresh flat-leaf parsley
salt and freshly ground black pepper

For the sauce
125ml (4fl oz) olive oil
2 leeks, trimmed and finely chopped
2 garlic cloves, peeled and finely chopped
1kg (2¼lb) fresh clams in shell
4 king scallops, fresh or frozen, shelled and cut in half horizontally
225ml (8fl oz) white wine
225ml (8fl oz) vegetable or fish stock

- Bring a large pan of salted water to the boil. Add the pasta and cook for 5–8 minutes, or according to the instructions on the packet, until *al dente*.
- Meanwhile, make the sauce. In another large pan heat 45ml (3 tablespoons) of the olive oil, stir in the leeks and garlic and fry for 3–5 minutes until golden. Add the clams and cook for 3 minutes until they open. Add the scallops, and stir in the wine and some of the stock. Bring to the boil, then reduce the heat and simmer for 5 minutes.
- Drain the pasta and add to the sauce, tossing well to mix. Add a little more stock to moisten, if necessary. Add the basil, parsley and remaining olive oil. Season well with salt and freshly ground black pepper. Serve immediately, with more freshly ground black pepper.

Maccheroncini alla Bolognese
Baby macaroni with traditional Bolognese sauce

Pecorino is a sharp cheese that can be either mild or very strong in taste. With Bolognese sauce I recommend a strong pecorino. You will find that it works far better than Parmesan. Although beef is normally used for Bolognese, in Italy pork is often an alternative. One of my regular customers, Brian Wiseman, visits Signor Zilli just to eat this dish.

Serves 4
Preparation time: 15 minutes
Cooking time: 10 minutes

350g (12oz) maccherocini pasta
1 quantity Ragù alla Bolognese (see page 204)
50g (2oz) butter
salt and freshly ground black pepper
60ml (4 tablespoons) freshly grated pecorino cheese

- Bring a large pan of salted water to the boil. Add the pasta and cook for 8–10 minutes, or according to the instructions on the packet, until *al dente*.
- Meanwhile, heat through the Bolognese sauce, then stir in the butter. Adjust seasoning to taste with salt and freshly ground black pepper.
- Drain the pasta and transfer to a large pasta bowl. Pour the sauce over the pasta and sprinkle with the pecorino cheese. Toss well to mix and serve.

Rigatoni del Fruttivendolo
Roast vegetable and rigatoni bake

My wife Jan invented this recipe. It can be made in advance and then frozen – once assembled (but not baked), cool and then freeze. Cook straight from the freezer for 45–50 mintues. If you use a vegetarian Parmesan, it makes a great vegetarian dish. The vegetables here can be varied, according to your taste and what is in season, so don't be afraid to experiment.

Serves 4
Preparation time: 25 minutes
Cooking time: 40 minutes

1.4kg (3lb) mixed vegetables, such as aubergines, courgettes, red onions, tomatoes, red and
    green peppers and mushrooms
60ml (4 tablespoons) olive oil
salt and freshly ground black pepper
350g (12oz) large rigatoni pasta
30ml (2 tablespoons) chopped fresh flat-leaf parsley
15ml (1 tablespoon) fresh thyme leaves
15ml (1 tablespoon) chopped fresh sage leaves
300ml (10fl oz) Salsa Besciamella (see page 206)
1 x 125g (5oz) mozzarella cheese, chopped
150g (5oz) Parmesan cheese, freshly grated

- Pre-heat the oven to 200°C, 400°F, Gas Mark 6. Cut all the vegetables into large chunks and spread out in 1 or 2 large baking trays. Drizzle over the oil and season with salt and freshly ground black pepper. Roast the vegetables for 15–20 minutes until tender and just beginning to brown in places.
- Meanwhile, cook the pasta in a large pan of boiling salted water for 10–12 minutes, or according to the instructions on the packet, until *al dente*. Drain.
- Mix the roast vegetables with the pasta and herbs, then place in an oblong baking dish.
- Reheat the béchamel sauce, if necessary. Stir the mozzarella into the hot sauce until the cheese melts, then adjust the seasoning, if necessary. Pour over the pasta and vegetables. Sprinkle with the Parmesan cheese.
- Place the dish on a baking sheet and bake for 20 minutes until the top is golden brown and crisp and the sauce is bubbling in places. Leave to rest for 5 minutes before serving.

Tagliatelle al Ragù di Salsiccia
Tagliatelle with Italian sausage sauce

For an excellent tasting sauce, be sure to use fresh sausages from a butcher or a good Italian deli. The sauce will keep for 3–4 days in the refrigerator, so you can make more than you need and then enjoy the remainder another day with a different pasta. If possible, make your own pasta – it's very rewarding and tastes fantastic.

Serves 4
Preparation time: 15 minutes
Cooking time: 1 hour 20 minutes

350g (12oz) fresh spinach or egg tagliatelle (see page 214 for home-made tagliatelle)
60ml (4 tablespoons) freshly grated pecorino or Parmesan cheese

For the sauce
8 fresh Italian pork and garlic sausages
15ml (1 tablespoon) olive oil
1 onion, peeled and finely chopped
1 carrot, peeled and finely chopped
1 celery stick, finely chopped
225ml (8fl oz) vegetable stock
2 flat mushrooms, chopped
1 bunch of fresh thyme, tough stalks removed
1 x 800g (1¾lb) can plum tomatoes
salt and freshly ground black pepper
50g (2oz) butter

- Pre-heat the oven to 200°C, 400°F, Gas Mark 6. Place the sausages on a baking tray and cook in the oven for 10 minutes.
- Heat the oil in a large saucepan, add the onion, carrot and celery and pour in the stock. Cook for 5 minutes. Chop the sausages and add to the pan together with the chopped mushrooms. Cook for a further 5 minutes. Stir in the thyme leaves and tomatoes with their juice. Season with salt and freshly ground black pepper. Cover and cook for 1 hour until the sauce is thick, stirring occasionally.
- During the final 10 minutes of the sauce's cooking time, cook the pasta in a large pan of boiling salted water for 5–8 minutes, or according to the instructions on the packet, until *al dente*. Drain and transfer to a large pasta bowl. Stir the butter into the sauce, then pour over the pasta. Sprinkle with the cheese and toss to mix. Serve immediately.

Spaghetti all'Astice
Spaghetti with fresh lobster

This is my signature dish at Zilli Fish and is definitely one that I cannot imagine ever removing from the menu. Everyone loves it. It tastes so good, and because people don't eat lobster very often it makes them feel that they are having a special treat. I buy live lobsters every day and amazingly manage to get through around 250 each week. Although I would recommend using fresh lobsters, frozen lobster meat can also be used. This is a particularly favourite dish with Les Dennis whenever he visits the restaurant.

Serves 2
Preparation time: 30 minutes
Cooking time: 15 minutes

175g (6oz) spaghetti
sprigs of fresh basil, to garnish

For the sauce
1 x 900g (2lb) cooked lobster (or use 2 smaller lobsters)
2 beef tomatoes, skinned and seeded
60ml (4 tablespoons) chopped fresh flat-leaf parsley
60ml (4 tablespoons) chopped fresh basil
2 garlic cloves, peeled and finely chopped
salt and freshly ground black pepper
50ml (2fl oz) olive oil
1 small red onion, peeled and finely chopped
50ml (2fl oz) brandy
150ml (5fl oz) dry white wine

- Split the lobster in half lengthways and break off the claws. Gently remove the lobster meat from the shells, trying to keep the claw meat intact; chop the body meat. If you like, wash the lobster body shells and set aside to use for presentation.
- Chop the tomato flesh and place in a bowl with the parsley, basil and half of the garlic. Season with salt and freshly ground black pepper. Set aside.
- In a large frying pan heat half of the oil and add the onion and remaining garlic. Stir in the lobster meat and pour over the brandy; ignite the alcohol to flambé. Once the flames have died down, add the tomato mixture together with the wine. Simmer for 5–8 minutes until the juices reduce slightly.
- Meanwhile, cook the spaghetti in a large pan of boiling salted water for 5–8 minutes, or according to the instructions on the packet, until *al dente*. Drain and add to the lobster

sauce, tossing well to mix. Adjust the seasoning if necessary.

- If using the lobster shells for presentation, place on 2 large serving plates or bowls and top with the spaghetti, spooning over the sauce. Drizzle over the remaining oil and garnish with basil sprigs. Serve immediately.

Bucatini all'Aglio Affumicato e Peperoni
Jumbo spaghetti with oak-smoked garlic and sautéed pepper sauce

Bucatini is like very large spaghetti. As a child I loved bucatini with a tomato sauce - it was fun, if somewhat messy, to eat because it was so slippery. This recipe is not so messy. Smoked garlic, which has a much more delicate flavour than normal garlic, adds a fantastic taste to this dish.

Serves 6
Preparation time: 10 minutes
Cooking time: 10 minutes

450g (1lb) bucatini pasta
60ml (4 tablespoons) freshly grated pecorino or Parmesan cheese

For the sauce
3 peppers (1 red, 1 green and 1 yellow)
125ml (4fl oz) olive oil
2 oak-smoked garlic cloves, peeled and finely chopped
2 bay leaves
2 bunches of fresh basil, stalks discarded and leaves shredded
50g (2oz) stoned black olives, chopped
25g (1oz) butter
salt and freshly ground black pepper

- Remove the stalks and seeds from all the peppers, then slice them thinly.
- Heat the oil in a large saucepan and add the sliced peppers, garlic and bay leaves. Cook for 3 minutes. Stir in the basil, olives and butter, and season with salt and freshly ground black pepper. Cook for 5–8 minutes, stirring occasionally.
- Meanwhile, cook the pasta in a large pan of boiling salted water for 5–8 minutes, or according to the instructions on the packet, until *al dente*. Drain, reserving a little of the cooking liquid.
- Add the pasta to the sauce, moistening with the reserved cooking liquid, if necessary. Add the cheese and stir well. Serve immediately, with more freshly ground black pepper.

Orecchiette alle Erbe e Rucola
Orecchiette pasta with herbs and rocket

'Orecchiette' in Italian means 'little ears', so that gives a clue to the shape of this pasta. It is a particularly good pasta for vegetable sauces as it captures the vegetables in its curves. This is a brilliant, quick and easy dish for vegetarians, and light and healthy too. It's a favourite with ex-model Huggy, who's now a supermodel photographer. If wild rocket is not available, you can use cultivated.

Serves 4
Preparation time: 10 minutes
Cooking time: 15 minutes

350g (12oz) orecchiette pasta
225g (8oz) wild rocket, trimmed
75ml (5 tablespoons) olive oil
2 garlic cloves, peeled and finely chopped
60ml (4 tablespoons) chopped fresh flat-leaf parsley
6 fresh basil leaves, roughly torn
2 fresh red chillies, seeded and cut into rings
salt and freshly ground black pepper
freshly grated pecorino cheese, to serve

- Bring a large pan of salted water to the boil. Add the pasta and cook for 5–8 minutes, or according to the instructions on the packet, until *al dente*.
- Meanwhile, blanch the rocket in a separate pan of boiling water for 4 minutes. Drain and refresh, then chop roughly.
- Heat 45ml (3 tablespoons) of the oil in a large frying pan and add the garlic, parsley and basil. Fry for 3 minutes, stirring frequently. Stir in the rocket and chillies and cook for a further 3 minutes.
- Drain the pasta, reserving 60ml (4 tablespoons) of the cooking liquid. Return the pasta and reserved liquid to the hot pan and add the herb mixture, tossing to mix. Season well with salt and freshly ground black pepper.
- Divide among 4 warmed serving bowls and drizzle with the remaining oil. Serve with grated pecorino cheese.

Risotto al Finocchio
Wild fennel risotto

Wild fennel is a very bright green and comes in long stems, looking like a very slim celery. It has an intense aniseed flavour, stronger than that of conventional bulb or Florence fennel. If you cannot find wild fennel, use cultivated fennel – you'll need about 2 bulbs of medium size.

Serves 4
Preparation time: 20 minutes
Cooking time: 20–25 minutes

75g (3oz) butter
1 onion, peeled and finely chopped
3–4 small heads of wild fennel, trimmed and finely sliced
350g (12oz) risotto rice
1.5 litres (2½ pints) hot vegetable stock
salt and freshly ground black pepper
100g (4oz) Parmesan cheese, freshly grated

- Melt 50g (2oz) of the butter in a deep pan and add the onion and fennel. Sauté for 5–8 minutes until the fennel is half cooked. Stir in the rice and cook for a few seconds.
- Gradually add the stock, a ladleful at a time, stirring and adding more stock as each batch is absorbed. The total cooking time will be about 20 minutes, at the end of which the rice should be *al dente*. Season to taste with salt and freshly ground black pepper.
- Stir the remaining butter into the risotto together with three-quarters of the Parmesan cheese. Allow the risotto to rest for 2–3 minutes, then serve with the remaining Parmesan cheese and more freshly ground black pepper.

Risotto alle Vongole e Seppie
Cuttlefish and clam risotto

This is quite an unusual recipe, but I find that the combination of flavours works beautifully. It is a particularly popular dish in my fish restaurant. Cuttlefish has more flavour than squid and is generally cheaper, but is not very common in this country. A good tip when cooking cuttlefish is to add a wine cork to the pan as it helps to tenderise the fish. The cuttlefish ink can be bought in separate sacs from good fishmongers.

Serves 4
Preparation time: 30 minutes
Cooking time: 50 minutes

800g (1¾lb) fresh clams in shell
450g (1lb) cuttlefish or squid
75ml (5 tablespoons) olive oil
1 onion, peeled and chopped
2 garlic cloves, peeled and chopped
60ml (4 tablespoons) chopped fresh flat-leaf parsley
350g (12oz) risotto rice
1.5 litres (2½ pints) hot fish stock
salt and freshly ground black pepper

- Rinse the clams and leave to soak in cold water for 30 minutes. Meanwhile, clean the cuttlefish carefully, discarding everything except the black ink sacs, and wash thoroughly. Cut the cuttlefish into small pieces, reserving the ink sacs.
- Drain the clams; discard any that remain open when lightly tapped on a hard surface. Place the clams in a large pan, cover tightly and cook gently for 3–5 minutes until all the clams open (discard any that remain closed). Drain the clams in a colander, reserving all the liquor. Discard the clam shells. Set aside the shelled clams and strained liquor until required.
- In a clean pan, heat the oil and stir in the onion, garlic and 45ml (3 tablespoons) of the parsley. Cook for 3–5 minutes until the onions are just golden. Stir in the cuttlefish and cook for 20 minutes.
- Add the rice to the pan together with the reserved clam liquor. Simmer, stirring, for 2 minutes. Gradually add the stock, a ladleful at a time, stirring and adding more stock as each batch is absorbed. Add the ink sacs half way through, and the shelled clams for the last 5 minutes. The total cooking time will be about 20 minutes, at the end of which the rice should be *al dente*.
- Season well with salt and freshly ground black pepper to taste. Serve immediately sprinkled with the remaining chopped parsley.

Risotto al Latte, Formaggio e Rucola
Milk, Parmesan and rocket risotto

The great thing about this quick and inexpensive risotto is that you can vary it easily. For example, you can add other cheese (50g/2oz per person), such as Gorgonzola or taleggio, and a slice of Parma ham per person (cut into strips), which will give the risotto a greater depth of flavour. If wild rocket is not available, use cultivated.

Serves 4
Preparation time: 20 minutes
Cooking time: 20–25 minutes

75g (3oz) butter
400g (14oz) risotto rice
75ml (3fl oz) white wine
1.5 litres (2½ pints) milk, warmed
50g (2oz) Parmesan cheese, freshly grated
1 x 125g (5oz) mozzarella cheese, drained and cubed
salt and freshly ground black pepper
225g (8oz) wild rocket, roughly chopped

- Melt 50g (2oz) of the butter in a deep pan and add the rice. Cook for 1 minute, stirring constantly. Add the wine and simmer, stirring constantly, until the wine is absorbed.
- Gradually add the milk, a ladleful at a time, stirring and adding more as each batch is aborbed. The total cooking time will be about 20 minutes, at the end of which the rice should be *al dente*.
- Stir in the Parmesan and mozzarella cheeses and cook for 2–3 minutes to melt the cheeses. Season to taste with salt and freshly ground black pepper.
- Stir in the remaining butter and serve the risotto immediately with the rocket sprinkled over the top.

Risotto Boscaiolo
Fruits of the forest risotto

In Italy at the moment it is very fashionable to use fruit with risotto, and believe me, it is delicious. I cooked this recipe when filming my TV show, The Italian Job, *and everyone loved it. This recipe can be adapted to make a dessert simply by omitting the leeks and using plain water instead of stock.*

Serves 4
Preparation time: 20 minutes
Cooking time: 25–30 minutes

3 leeks, trimmed and finely chopped
60ml (4 tablespoons) brown sugar
15ml (1 tablespoon) olive oil
100g (4oz) butter
60ml (4 tablespoons) lime juice
300g (11oz) risotto rice
150ml (5fl oz) sweet vermouth
150ml (5fl oz) dessert wine
1.5 litres (2½ pints) hot vegetable stock
450g (1lb) mixed berries, such as raspberries, small strawberries, blackberries and blueberries, washed and drained well
25g (1oz) fresh mint, stalks removed

- Bring a large pan of water to the boil. Add the leeks and 15ml (1 tablespoon) of the brown sugar and cook for 2 minutes. Drain.
- In another large pan, heat the oil and add the drained leeks, 25g (1oz) of the butter and 30ml (2 tablespoons) of the remaining brown sugar. Cook gently for 3–5 minutes until the leeks are golden brown. Stir in the lime juice.
- Add the rice to the leeks, stir well and cook for 1 minute. Add the vermouth, wine and 1–2 ladlefuls of stock. Add three-quarters of the berries and stir gently, then simmer until the liquid has been absorbed. Continue adding the stock, 1–2 ladlefuls at a time, stirring and adding more as each batch is absorbed. The total cooking time will be about 20 minutes. When finished, the risotto should be wet but not runny and the grains of rice *al dente*.
- Meanwhile, heat 25g (1oz) of the remaining butter in a pan and add the remaining berries and brown sugar. Cook gently until the berries soften and can be mashed into a coulis.
- Add the remaining butter and three-quarters of the mint leaves to the risotto. To serve, place 30ml (2 tablespoons) coulis on each of 4 warmed serving plates, then spoon over the risotto and garnish with the remaining mint leaves.

Risotto d'Orzo e Porcini in Gabbia
Wild mushroom and barley risotto in Parmesan baskets

Parmesan cheese baskets are extremely easy to make and brilliant for presentation (turn to the photograph to see how spectacular they look). For a dinner party, your guests could not fail to be impressed by your culinary skills. One of my oldest chums and a regular customer, Tom Gutteridge, loves good food and the good life. He is now learning to cook, so I expect that he'll soon be able to create this wonderful dish at home. If you prefer, use another of my risottos to fill the baskets. If you cannot get fresh porcini, use a mixture of dried porcini (soaked) and fresh chestnut mushrooms.

Serves 4
Preparation time: 30 minutes
Cooking time: 50 minutes–1 hour

For the Parmesan baskets
25g (1oz) fine polenta flour
50g (2oz) Parmesan cheese, freshly grated

For the risotto
50g (2oz) butter
1 small onion, peeled and finely chopped
450g (1lb) fresh porcini, wiped clean and sliced
300g (11oz) pearl barley
1 sprig of fresh rosemary, stalk discarded and leaves finely chopped
150ml (5fl oz) dry white wine
1.5 litres (2½ pints) hot vegetable stock
1 bunch of fresh chives, snipped
salt and freshly ground black pepper
shavings of Parmesan cheese, to serve

- Make one Parmesan cheese basket at a time. Pre-heat the grill. Sprinkle one-quarter of the polenta in a fine, even layer over the bottom of a non-stick pan. Cover with one-quarter of the Parmesan cheese. Cook over a high heat for 2 minutes, then place under the hot grill for 2 minutes to cook the top. Remove the 'pancake' from the pan and drape over an upturned sugar bowl to give a basket shape. Repeat with the remaining polenta and Parmesan to make 4 baskets in total. Leave until cold and set before removing from the bowls.

- To make the risotto, melt 15g (½oz) of the butter in a large pan and add the onion. Cover with dampened greaseproof paper (the paper should touch the onion), then put on the lid. Cook (sweat) the onion for 5 minutes until soft but not coloured.
- Stir the porcini, barley and rosemary into the onion and cook for 2 minutes. Stir in the wine and simmer until the wine has been absorbed. Gradually add the stock, a ladleful at a time, stirring and adding more stock as each addition is absorbed. The total cooking time will be 30–40 minutes.
- Stir the chives and remaining butter into the risotto, and season well with salt and freshly ground black pepper.
- Place the Parmesan baskets on individual serving plates and spoon the risotto into them. Garnish with Parmesan cheese shavings and serve with more freshly ground black pepper.

Risotto agli Asparagi
Asparagus and mascarpone risotto

I love cooking with mascarpone – it's great for both sweet and savoury dishes. There are many different varieties of asparagus, but English asparagus in season is my favourite. Martin and Shirley were great fans of this dish when I first put it on the menu.

Serves 4
Preparation time: 20 minutes
Cooking time: 25 minutes

30ml (2 tablespoons) olive oil
1 small red onion, peeled and finely chopped
350g (12oz) risotto rice
900g (2lb) thin English asparagus spears, 4 kept whole and the remainder chopped
1.5 litres (2½ pints) hot vegetable stock
salt and freshly ground black pepper
50g (2oz) butter
125g (4oz) mascarpone cheese
75g (3oz) Parmesan cheese, freshly grated

- Heat the oil in a large pan, add the onion and fry for 2–3 minutes until just golden. Stir in the rice and chopped asparagus and cook for a few more seconds.
- Gradually add the stock, a ladleful at a time, stirring and adding more stock as each batch is absorbed. The total cooking time will be about 20 minutes, at the end of which the rice should be *al dente*.
- Meanwhile, blanch the whole asparagus spears in a pan of boiling water for 2–3 minutes until just tender and bright green. Refresh with cold water, then thinly slice each asparagus spear lengthways into a fan. Set aside.
- Season the risotto to taste with salt and freshly ground black pepper. Stir in the butter, mascarpone and three-quarters of the Parmesan cheese. Leave to rest for 2 minutes.
- Spoon the risotto on to 4 warmed serving plates and garnish with the asparagus fans placed on top. Serve with the remaining Parmesan cheese and more freshly ground black pepper.

Risotto Vecchia Romagna
Risotto with chicken, Parma ham and brandy

This is a very substantial risotto using both chicken and ham, so serve it in small portions as a starter or enjoy it as a main course. For a family meal just omit the brandy.

Serves 4
Preparation time: 20 minutes
Cooking time: 25–30 minutes

75g (3oz) butter
1 onion, peeled and finely chopped
100g (4oz) boneless chicken breast, skinned and chopped
50g (2oz) Parma ham, chopped
125ml (4fl oz) Italian brandy
75ml (3fl oz) dry white wine
350g (12oz) risotto rice
1.2 litres (2 pints) hot chicken stock
225ml (8fl oz) single cream, warmed
salt and freshly ground black pepper
50g (2oz) Parmesan cheese, freshly grated

- Heat 50g (2oz) of the butter in a large deep pan, add the onion and sauté for 3–5 minutes until the onion is golden. Stir in the chicken and Parma ham. Add the brandy and ignite to flambé. Once the flames have died down add the wine and cook for 2–3 minutes.
- Stir in the rice and cook for a few more seconds. Gradually add the stock, a ladleful at a time, stirring and adding more stock as each batch is absorbed. The total cooking time will be about 15 minutes.
- Gradually add the cream to the risotto. The rice should be *al dente*. Season to taste with salt and freshly ground black pepper, and stir in the the Parmesan cheese and the remaining butter. Remove from the heat and continue to stir for 2 minutes. Serve.

Risotto alle Cape Sante
Fresh scallop risotto

This is my favourite risotto as I adore scallops. I would choose diver-picked king scallops, which are more environmentally friendly than dredged scallops. Although they are expensive they are absolutely superb. A good alternative to scallops is monkfish, cut into large chunks. Simply griddle or pan-fry as you would the scallops and add to the risotto. This risotto is a winner with David Austin and with Derek and Pepsi, who always shower me with compliments when they eat this.

Serves 4
Preparation time: 20 minutes
Cooking time: 30–35 minutes

50g (2oz) butter
4 shallots, peeled and finely chopped
350g (12oz) risotto rice
300ml (10fl oz) dry white wine
1.5 litres (2½ pints) hot vegetable stock
1 small onion, peeled and finely sliced into rings
1 small carrot, peeled and cut into thin sticks
40g (1½oz) baby spinach, roughly shredded
50g (2oz) plain flour
vegetable oil for deep-frying
60ml (4 tablespoons) olive oil
150g (5oz) shelled scallops, fresh or frozen, patted dry on kitchen paper
salt and freshly ground black pepper

- Melt the butter in a large deep pan, add the shallots and sauté for 3–5 minutes until golden. Stir in the rice and cook for a few more seconds. Add the wine and simmer for 5 minutes, stirring, until the wine is absorbed.
- Gradually add the stock, a ladleful at a time, stirring and adding more stock as each batch is absorbed. The total cooking time will be about 20 minutes, at the end of which the rice should be *al dente*.
- Meanwhile, mix together the onion, carrot and spinach on a plate, then toss in the flour. Heat vegetable oil in a small deep pan until a piece of vegetable dropped into the oil sizzles immediately. Gently add the floured vegetables and deep-fry for 3–5 minutes until crisp. Remove and drain on kitchen paper.
- Heat the olive oil in a frying pan until very hot and almost smoking. Add the scallops. Sear for 2 minutes on each side until golden brown.

- Season the risotto to taste with salt and freshly ground black pepper. Spoon the risotto on to 4 warmed serving plates and top with the scallops and crisp vegetables. Serve with more freshly ground black pepper.

Easter. Top left: *Rollatini di Scamorza al Prosciutto con Pera e Radicchio* (page 94); top right: *Timballo Abruzzese* (page 95); bottom left: *Carrè d'Agnello al Rosmarino* (page 97)

Ferragosto. Top left: *Zuppa di Fiori di Zucchini* (page 102); top right: *Spaghetti Scoglio* (page 103); bottom right: *Orata al Cartoccio* (page 105)

Top left: *Peperoni Ripieni* (page 53); top right: *Finocchio Rosolato* (page 130);
bottom left: *Rollatini di Melanzane* (page 56)

Top left: *Tiramisù del Boscaiolo* (page 81); top right: *Panna Cotta al Cioccolato* (page 82);
bottom right: *Tagliolini al Gelato* (page 84)

Risotto di Salvia e Pancetta
Sage, pancetta and sweetcorn risotto

You can easily replace the pancetta with smoked bacon, or, if you're cooking for a vegetarian, leave out the pancetta or bacon altogether. The sage, sweetcorn and pecorino will still provide plenty of flavour in this delicious risotto.

Serves 4
Preparation time: 20 minutes
Cooking time: 30 minutes

30ml (2 tablespoons) olive oil
50g (2oz) butter
2 shallots, peeled and finely chopped
100g (4oz) pancetta, diced
6 fresh sage leaves, finely chopped
350g (12oz) risotto rice
75ml (3fl oz) dry white wine
1.5 litres (2½ pints) hot vegetable stock
250g (9oz) sweetcorn kernels, fresh or frozen
salt and freshly ground black pepper
50g (2oz) pecorino cheese, freshly grated

- Heat the oil and 25g (1oz) of the butter in a deep pan, add the shallots, pancetta and sage, and sauté for 5 minutes until the shallots are golden brown. Stir in the rice and cook for a few more seconds. Add the wine and simmer for 3–5 minutes until the wine has been absorbed.
- Gradually add the stock, a ladleful at a time, stirring and adding more stock as each addition is absorbed. The total cooking time will be about 20 minutes, at the end of which the rice should be *al dente*. After half the stock has been added, stir in the sweetcorn.
- Season to taste with salt and freshly ground black pepper. Stir in the pecorino cheese together with the remaining butter. Serve immediately whilst still moist.

Risotto al Carciofo
Artichoke, mozzarella and herb risotto

When buying fresh artichokes, choose small young ones which will be more tender than large ones. If short on time, use artichoke hearts in brine - they're available in cans or jars in all good supermarkets and delis – but avoid those preserved in oil. Canned artichokes do not need to be cooked before being added to the risotto.

Serves 4
Preparation time: 40 minutes
Cooking time: 30 minutes

3 globe artichokes
juice of 1 lemon
50g (2oz) butter
2 garlic cloves, peeled and crushed
salt and freshly ground black pepper
1.5 litres (2½ pints) hot vegetable stock
350g (12oz) risotto rice
1 bunch of fresh flat-leaf parsley, tough stalks discarded and leaves chopped
200g (7oz) mozzarella cheese, cubed
15ml (1 tablespoon) freshly grated Parmesan cheese

- To prepare the artichokes: cut off the stalks, then cut off the tops and discard any tough leaves. Halve the artichokes lengthways through the middle and scoop out the choke with a teaspoon. Finely slice the artichokes lengthways and place in water with the lemon juice to prevent discoloration. Set aside until required.
- In a large frying pan, melt half of the butter and fry the garlic until it browns. Remove the garlic and discard. Drain the artichokes and add to the garlic-flavoured butter. Season with salt and freshly ground black pepper. Cook for 1 minute, then add 60–75ml (4–5 tablespoons) of the stock. Cook over a low heat for 10 minutes until the artichokes are tender.
- Add the rice to the artichokes together with a ladleful of stock and stir well. Once the stock has been absorbed, add another ladleful. Continue adding the stock, a ladleful at a time, stirring and adding more as each addition is absorbed. The total cooking time will be about 20 minutes.
- About 2 minutes before the rice is *al dente*, stir in the parsley and mozzarella. Top the risotto with the Parmesan cheese and remaining butter to serve.

Insalata Mare e Monti
Seafood and wild mushroom salad

My region of Abruzzo inspired this recipe title – the sea-side and mountains provide the two main ingredients for this stunning recipe. I was born in the mountains, but moved to a small village by the sea when I was a child. The sea can be seen from almost every point of this mountainous land.

Serves 4
Preparation time: 10 minutes
Cooking time: 10–15 minutes

150g (5oz) mussels, cleaned
150g (5oz) clams, cleaned
150g (5oz) cleaned squid bodies, cut into rings
150ml (5fl oz) dry white wine
30ml (2 tablespoons) chopped fresh flat-leaf parsley
150g (5oz) cooked peeled prawns
60ml (4 tablespoons) olive oil
1 onion, peeled and chopped
2 garlic cloves, peeled and crushed
225g (8oz) fresh wild mushrooms, such as oyster, porcini or girolles, wiped clean and cut
    lengthways
4 drops of Tabasco sauce
juice of ½ lemon
45ml (3 tablespoons) chopped fresh chervil
salt and freshly ground black pepper

- Place the mussels, clams and squid rings in a large pan with the wine and parsley. Cover and bring to the boil. Cook for 2–3 minutes until the squid rings are tender and the shells of the mussels and clams are open (discard any mussels or clams that remain closed). Stir in the prawns, then remove from the heat and allow to cool.
- In another pan combine the oil, onion and garlic. Cover with a damp piece of greaseproof paper (the paper should touch the onion), put on the lid and sweat for 5 minutes until soft. Remove the paper and lid. Add the mushrooms and fry for 5–6 minutes until tender. Remove from the heat and allow to cool.
- Place the mussel mixture in a large bowl with the mushrooms. Add the Tabasco, lemon juice and chervil and season well with salt and freshly ground black pepper. Mix well and serve immediately.

Bufala, Ruchetta e Peperoni
Buffalo mozzarella, wild baby rocket and roasted pepper salad

The colours of the Italian flag are the inspiration for this simple yet beautiful salad. I find that it is a good variation on the traditional mozzarella and avocado version. When she can, Naomi Campbell visits my Dean Street restaurant, in between her modelling assignments, and this is a dish she loves.

Serves 4
Preparation time: 15 minutes
Cooking time: 20 minutes

3 peppers (red and yellow only)
60ml (4 tablespoons) olive oil
2 sprigs of fresh rosemary
15ml (1 tablespoon) capers
salt and freshly ground black pepper
225g (8oz) rocket, preferably wild
4 x 125g (5oz) buffalo mozzarella cheeses, drained and halved

To serve
extra virgin olive oil
flaked sea salt

- Pre-heat the oven to 180°C, 350°F, Gas Mark 4. Place the whole peppers on a baking tray, drizzle over some of the oil and add 1 sprig of rosemary. Roast for 20 minutes until the skins are just charred all over and the peppers are soft to the touch. Place the peppers in a plastic bag and set aside to cool. Transfer the cooking juices to a small bowl and reserve.
- Cut the tops from the peppers and remove the seeds and membranes; peel off the skin. Slice the flesh into strips and place in a large bowl. Remove the stalk from the remaining rosemary sprig and add the leaves to the peppers together with the capers, reserved cooking juices and any remaining olive oil. Season to taste with salt and freshly ground black pepper.
- Arrange the rocket and roasted peppers on individual serving plates. Place 2 mozzarella halves on each plate. Drizzle with extra virgin olive oil and season well with flaked sea salt and freshly ground black pepper.

Stufato di Scarola, Porcini e Parmigiano
Steamed escarole, porcini and Parmesan salad

This salad is a great accompaniment for roasts. If escarole lettuce is not available, use frisée or curly endive.

Serves 4
Preparation time: 10 minutes
Cooking time: 8 minutes

175g (6oz) fresh porcini, wiped clean and stalks trimmed
175g (6oz) escarole, large leaves discarded
60ml (4 tablespoons) olive oil
15ml (1 tablespoon) balsamic vinegar
45ml (3 tablespoons) chopped fresh flat-leaf parsley
salt and freshly ground black pepper
175g (6oz) rocket
50g (2oz) fresh Parmesan cheese shavings
30ml (2 tablespoons) pine nuts, toasted (optional)

- Either set up a steamer or set a metal sieve over a pan of boiling water. Place the porcini in the steamer or sieve, cover and steam for 8 minutes until tender. Add the escarole after 4 minutes. Remove and set aside to cool. Slice the porcini.
- Mix the olive oil and vinegar in a bowl with the parsley and season with salt and freshly ground black pepper.
- Place the rocket leaves and steamed escarole in a large serving bowl. Add the dressing and mix together gently. Place the Parmesan shavings and porcini on top and sprinkle over the pine nuts. Serve within 15 minutes, otherwise the leaves will become soggy.

Salads

Salads

Insalata Primavera
Baby sweetcorn, radicchio, chicory and red onion salad

An excellent salad, this makes a good accompaniment to fish and chicken dishes. You can use other baby vegetables in season, such as courgettes, carrots and leeks.

Serves 4
Preparation time: 5 minutes
Cooking time: 5 minutes

225g (8oz) baby sweetcorn
75ml (5 tablespoons) olive oil
35ml (2½ tablespoons) red wine vinegar
juice from a wedge of lime
45ml (3 tablespoons) chopped fresh basil leaves
45ml (3 tablespoons) chopped fresh flat-leaf parsley
1 red onion, peeled and finely chopped
salt and freshly ground black pepper
1 red Treviso chicory or radicchio, leaves separated
2 heads of chicory, leaves separated

- Blanch the baby sweetcorn in boiling water for 5 minutes. Drain and refresh under cold water.
- Place the oil and vinegar in a small bowl with the lime juice, basil, parsley and onion. Mix well, then season with salt and freshly ground black pepper.
- Place the baby sweetcorn in a large bowl with the salad leaves. Pour over the dressing and gently toss to mix well, taking care not to bruise the delicate leaves. Serve immediately.

Caprino alla Pera
Salad of poached pear with grilled goat's cheese

A hard goat's cheese is best for this salad. Italian caprino (goat's cheese) is too soft, so I would recommend using a goat's cheese from Wales. The poached pears can be prepared in advance (the day before) and kept, covered in the poaching liquid, in the refrigerator.

Serves 6
Preparation time: 15 minutes
Cooking time: 10 minutes

225g (8oz) caster sugar
grated zest and juice of 2 oranges
grated zest and juice of 2 lemons
2 whole cloves
1 bay leaf
1 cinnamon stick
600ml (1 pint) white wine
600ml (1 pint) water
6 pears, peeled, halved and cored with stalks left intact
225g (8oz) rocket
60ml (4 tablespoons) olive oil
15ml (1 tablespoon) balsamic vinegar
salt and freshly ground black pepper
600g (1¼lb) goat's cheese, cut into 6 equal rounds

- Place the sugar in a large saucepan with the orange and lemon zest and juices, cloves, bay leaf, cinnamon stick, wine and water. Gently heat until the sugar dissolves. Add the pears and bring to the boil. Cover with greaseproof paper (the paper should touch the pears) and poach for 4–5 minutes until soft to the touch. Drain the pears on kitchen paper.
- Place the rocket in a bowl and dress with the olive oil and balsamic vinegar, then season with salt and freshly ground black pepper. Divide among 6 serving plates.
- Pre-heat the grill to medium-hot. Place each round of goat's cheese between 2 pear halves and arrange on a foil-lined grill pan. Season with salt and freshly ground black pepper. Grill the pears for 3–4 minutes until the cheese just begins to melt. Quickly lift on to the rocket. Serve immediately.

Spinaci alla Pancetta e Funghi
Baby spinach, pancetta and mushroom salad

Add some avocado and you can turn this into a great starter. If pancetta is not available, smoked bacon will do.

Serves 4
Preparation time: 10 minutes

8 thin slices of pancetta
450g (1lb) baby spinach leaves, tough stalks removed then washed and dried with kitchen
    paper
225g (8oz) button mushrooms, wiped clean and thinly sliced
90ml (6 tablespoons) olive oil
45ml (3 tablespoons) cider vinegar
2 garlic cloves, peeled and crushed
15ml (1 tablespoon) Dijon mustard
10ml (2 teaspoons) mascarpone cheese
salt and freshly ground black pepper

- Thinly slice the pancetta into ribbons and mix with the spinach and mushrooms in a large bowl.
- Place the oil in a blender and add the vinegar, garlic, mustard and mascarpone. Season with salt and freshly ground black pepper. Process until the dressing is smooth and creamy.
- Spoon the dressing over the salad mixture and toss to mix well. Adjust the seasoning to taste, then serve immediately.

Mango al Granchio
Crab meat, mango and endive salad

The meat from a fresh crab, bought from a fishmonger, will make a tastier salad than frozen crabmeat. The crab will be cooked and may already be 'dressed' (the meat will have been removed from the claws and shell and placed in the body cavity).

Serves 4
Preparation time: 15 minutes

1 ripe mango
275g (10oz) crabmeat, thawed if frozen
5ml (1 teaspoon) grated fresh root ginger
2 spring onions, trimmed and finely chopped
salt and freshly ground black pepper
60ml (4 tablespoons) olive oil
juice of 1 lime
1 curly endive (frisée), leaves separated

- Peel the mango and remove the stone. Finely dice the mango flesh. Reserve one-quarter of the mango for garnish, and place the remainder in a bowl. Add the crabmeat, ginger and spring onions and season with salt and freshly ground black pepper. Mix together well.
- In a small bowl, mix the olive oil and lime juice to make a dressing. Place the endive leaves in a bowl and gently toss with the dressing.
- Spoon the mango and crabmeat mixture on to the endive leaves. Top with the reserved diced mango and serve.

Gorgonzola al Finocchio
Gorgonzola, fennel and carrot salad

Fennel is one of the main vegetables in Italy, and makes a crunchy and refreshing addition to a salad. You could use taleggio, dolcelatte or Parmesan cheese in place of Gorgonzola, if you don't like its strong taste. However, I find that Gorgonzola works very well with fennel.

Serves 4
Preparation time: 15 minutes
Cooking time: 10 minutes

2 medium carrots, peeled
2 fennel bulbs, trimmed
30ml (2 tablespoons) olive oil
2 onions, peeled and thinly sliced
225g (8oz) Gorgonzola cheese, cut into cubes
salt and freshly ground black pepper

- Using a potato peeler, slice the carrots lengthways to give ribbons. Finely slice the fennel.
- Bring a large pan of water to the boil and add the fennel. Blanch for 2 minutes, then add the carrots and blanch for another 2 minutes. Drain and refresh under cold water.
- Heat the oil in a frying pan, add the onions and cook for 5 minutes until just beginning to brown. Remove from the heat and allow to cool.
- Add the carrots and fennel to the onions and stir to coat the vegetables with oil. Stir in the Gorgonzola and season with salt and freshly ground black pepper to taste. Drizzle with a little extra oil if too dry. Serve.

Insalata Quatro Fagioli
Four bean salad with tuna

For a healthier main course salad, use 350g (12oz) grilled fresh tuna in place of canned tuna.

Serves 4
Preparation time: 10 minutes
Cooking time: 5 minutes

100g (4oz) podded broad beans
100g (4oz) runner beans, trimmed and diagonally sliced
100g (4oz) French beans, trimmed and halved
1 x 400g (14oz) can borlotti beans, drained
1 large onion, peeled and thinly sliced into rings
30ml (2 tablespoons) roughly chopped fresh flat-leaf parsley
70ml (4½ tablespoons) olive oil
30ml (2 tablespoons) cider vinegar
juice of ½ lemon
2.5ml (½ teaspoon) honey
1 garlic clove, peeled and crushed
15ml (1 tablespoon) boiling water
salt and freshly ground black pepper
2 x 227g (7oz) cans tuna in brine, drained and flaked

- Bring a large pan of water to the boil. Add the broad beans and boil for 1 minute. Add the runner and French beans and boil for a further 4 minutes. Drain and refresh with cold water. Remove the tough outer skins from the broad beans, revealing the bright green, tender inner beans.
- Transfer all the green beans to a large bowl and mix in the borlotti beans, onion and half of the parsley.
- Mix the oil in a bowl with the vinegar, lemon juice, honey, garlic and water to make a vinaigrette. Season with salt and freshly ground black pepper. Pour the dressing over the bean mixture and toss well.
- Add the tuna and gently toss to mix. Transfer to a serving dish and sprinkle with the remaining parsley to serve.

Foglie alla Greca
Mixed leaf and feta salad

Although feta is, of course, not an Italian cheese, I'm including this super-fast salad especially for Susie Theodorou, the food stylist on this book. Susie is always rushing around and is never on time – except when there's a Greek salad on offer! This makes a great snack on a hot summer's day, and brings back memories of a romantic holiday in Greece.

Serves 4
Preparation time: 5 minutes

225g (8oz) mixed salad leaves, such as rocket, radicchio and lollo rosso
2 sprigs of fresh rosemary, stalks removed and leaves chopped
60ml (4 tablespoons) virgin olive oil
30ml (2 tablespoons) white wine vinegar
juice of ½ lime
2.5ml (½ teaspoon) caster sugar
2 garlic cloves, peeled and crushed
salt and freshly ground black pepper
275g (10oz) feta cheese, sliced
100g (4oz) black olives, stoned and quartered

- Tear the salad leaves into bite-size pieces and place in a large bowl. Add the rosemary leaves and toss to mix.
- To make the dressing, place the olive oil in a blender with the vinegar, lime juice, sugar and garlic and season with salt and freshly ground black pepper. Process until frothy.
- Pour the dressing over the salad leaves and toss to mix. Scatter the feta and olives over the leaves. Serve immediately.

Peperoni Ripieni
Stuffed red peppers

This title doesn't do this marvellous dish justice – stuffed peppers have moved into the 1990s. At home in Italy we used to grow peppers, and because they were so abundant my mother put them into almost everything. This is still my preferred way to cook peppers and it's a great vegetarian recipe – I've cooked it on many occasions for Linda McCartney.

Serves 4
Preparation time: 15 minutes
Cooking time: 50–55 minutes

50g (2oz) butter
2 garlic cloves, peeled and chopped
1 large onion, peeled and chopped
2 courgettes, trimmed and finely diced
1 x 400g (14oz) can plum tomatoes, drained
salt and freshly ground black pepper
30ml (2 tablespoons) balsamic vinegar
150g (5oz) long-grain rice, cooked
50g (2oz) stoned black olives, halved
15ml (1 tablespoon) chopped fresh oregano
15ml (1 tablespoon) chopped fresh marjoram
4 red peppers
olive oil for drizzling

- Pre-heat the oven to 180°C, 350°F, Gas Mark 4. Heat the butter in a large pan and add the garlic and onion. Gently fry for 3–5 minutes until the onion just begins to brown. Add the courgettes and tomatoes and season with salt and freshly ground black pepper. Bring to the boil, then simmer for 10–15 minutes until slightly thickened.
- Away from the heat, add the balsamic vinegar to the tomato mixture followed by the cooked rice, olives and herbs.
- Slice the stalk end from each pepper and reserve. Gently ease the seeds and ribs from the peppers and discard. Spoon the rice mixture into the peppers and stand them upright in a roasting tin, securing their position with crumpled foil. Place the reserved tops back on the peppers.
- Bake for 35 minutes. Drizzle a little oil over the peppers if they begin to dry out too much during cooking. The peppers should be softened and just beginning to brown in places. Serve warm or cold with salad.

Asparagi alla Parmigiana
Asparagus gratin with Parmesan

Asparagus is so delicious, especially when in season in the summer. The Romans considered it to be an aphrodisiac, so perhaps this dish should be served for a romantic dinner? For an extra special touch, melt some smoked mozzarella on top or wrap the asparagus in Parma ham. This also makes a brilliant starter.

Serves 4
Preparation time: 5 minutes
Cooking time: 15–20 minutes

450g (1lb) asparagus
juice of ½ lemon
100g (4oz) Parmesan cheese
5ml (1 teaspoon) freshly ground black pepper

- Trim the woody stalks of the asparagus. Fill a tall asparagus pan with water and bring to the boil. Place the asparagus, stalk end down, into the pan and simmer for 10–12 minutes, depending on the thickness of the asparagus spears. The tips of the asparagus must only be submerged for the final 2 minutes of cooking, othewise they will overcook and become slimy. Drain.
- Pre-heat the grill.
- Place the asparagus in a gratin dish and and sprinkle over the lemon juice. Grate 50g (2oz) of the Parmesan cheese on the coarse holes of a cheese grater, and gently stir through the asparagus.
- Slice the remaining Parmesan cheese into fine curls on the blade of a standard cheese grater. Scatter over the asparagus and sprinkle with the black pepper. Grill for 4–5 minutes until the cheese is bubbling and golden brown. Serve immediately with more freshly ground black pepper.

Patate Dolci al Forno
Baked sweet potatoes with leeks and mozzarella

Sweet potatoes are not used in central Italy, where I come from, but I tried them in dishes to serve in my restaurants and they have been a great success. I love simple mashed sweet potatoes with the Italian sausage casserole on page 135.

Serves 4
Preparation time: 10 minutes
Cooking time: 45 minutes

1.2kg (2½lb) sweet potatoes, peeled and thickly sliced
450g (1lb) leeks, trimmed and sliced into thick rings
3 x 125g (5oz) buffalo mozzarella cheeses, drained and thinly sliced
salt and freshly ground black pepper
300ml (10fl oz) vegetable stock
30ml (2 tablespoons) olive oil
25g (1oz) butter

- Pre-heat the oven to 180°C, 350°F, Gas Mark 4. Bring a large pan of water to the boil. Add the sweet potatoes and boil for 4 minutes. Drain.
- In a deep ovenproof dish, layer the sweet potato slices, leeks and mozzarella, seasoning between the layers with salt and freshly ground black pepper. Finish with a layer of sweet potatoes. Pour over the stock, then drizzle with the olive oil. Dot with the butter.
- Bake for 40 minutes until the sweet potatoes are tender and the top layer is golden and crisp. Serve immediately.

Rollatini di Melanzane
Rolled aubergine with sea salt and olive oil

These aubergine rolls are delicious served with a balsamic vinegar dressing as the dressing gives a sweet taste – use aged balsamic vinegar, about 25ml (5 teaspoons), to 70ml (scant 5 tablespoons) olive oil.

Serves 4
Preparation time: 20 minutes
Cooking time: 15 minutes

4 aubergines, trimmed and thinly sliced lengthways
75g (3oz) flaked sea salt
75ml (5 tablespoons) balsamic vinegar
30ml (2 tablespoons) olive oil
50g (2oz) butter, softened
50g (2oz) Parmesan cheese, freshly grated
freshly ground black pepper
stalks of fresh rosemary, leaves discarded, or wooden cocktail sticks, to secure
radicchio leaves, to garnish

- Place the aubergine slices in a colander and sprinkle over the salt. Set the colander on a plate and leave to stand for 10 minutes; the salt will draw out any bitter juices from the aubergines.
- Rinse the aubergines and pat dry on kitchen paper. Place in a dish, sprinkle over the balsamic vinegar and leave to marinate for 5 minutes.
- Pre-heat a ridged cast iron grill pan until almost smoking. Add the oil, then lay the aubergine slices on the pan and cook for 3–4 minutes, turning over half way through.
- In a small bowl, mix together the butter and Parmesan cheese and season with plenty of freshly ground black pepper. Make a small roll of the cheese mixture in your hands. Place it at one end of a slice of aubergine, roll up and secure with a stalk of rosemary or cocktail stick. Fill and roll the remaining aubergine slices.
- Pre-heat the grill. Place the aubergine rolls on a foil-lined grill pan and grill for 5–10 minutes until golden brown and crisp. Serve immediately with a garnish of radicchio leaves.

Zuppetta alla Pescarese
Fish soup Pescara-style

Pescara is a charming, traditional fishing town on the Adriatic coast, a few miles from my home. In the school holidays, I used to help the local fishmonger bring baskets of the fresh catch to the shop and in exchange he would give me lots of fish to take home to my mother to cook. I love to serve bruschetta *with fish in a broth or light sauce, because the bread can soak up all the delicious liquid. Simply rub slices of ciabatta bread with chopped garlic and then toast them in the oven. Virgin Radio's Russ Williams must be a fan of my food as he keeps promoting my restaurants on his show, and can often be found enjoying dishes such as this. Serve with a chilled dry white wine such as Verdicchio dei Castell Dijesi.*

Serves 6
Preparation time: 20 minutes
Cooking time: 30 minutes

1 medium Spanish onion, peeled
1 fennel bulb, trimmed
1 celery stick, trimmed
1 carrot, peeled
60ml (4 tablespoons) extra virgin olive oil
1 small fresh red chilli, seeded and finely chopped
2 garlic cloves, peeled and finely chopped
30ml (2 tablespoons) fresh thyme leaves, chopped
1 sprig of fresh rosemary, stalk discarded and leaves chopped
175ml (6fl oz) dry white wine
15ml (1 tablespoon) sugar
15ml (1 tablespoon) red wine vinegar
4 large beef tomatoes, skinned, seeded and chopped
1 litre (1¾ pints) fish stock
salt and freshly ground black pepper
1kg (2¼lb) mussels
1kg (2¼lb) clams
12 raw tiger prawns in shell
3 x 175g (6oz) red mullet, filleted and each fillet cut in half
6 x 100g (4oz) raw langoustines in shell
350g (12oz) fillet of white fish such as haddock, cut into 2.5cm (1in) pieces
1 bunch of fresh flat-leaf parsley, finely chopped

● Finely dice the onion, fennel, celery and carrot. Place all the vegetables in a large saucepan with the oil, chilli, garlic, thyme and rosemary. Place a piece of wet greaseproof paper directly on the vegetables, cover with the lid and cook over a very low heat for 10 minutes until the vegetables are very tender but not browned.

- Remove the lid and paper. Stir the wine into the vegetables together with the sugar and vinegar. Cook over a high heat for 5 minutes until the juices are quite syrupy. Add the tomatoes and fish stock and season with salt and freshly ground black pepper. Simmer for 15 minutes.

- Meanwhile, scrub clean the mussels and clams, removing any beards and barnacles. If any mussels or clams are open, tap them on a hard surface; if they remain open, discard them.

- Add the mussels and clams to the pan and cook for 5 minutes until the shells open. Add the prawns, red mullet fillets, langoustines and pieces of white fish. Simmer gently for 3–4 minutes until the fish and prawns are cooked. Adjust the seasoning to taste, stir in the parsley and serve immediately with *bruschetta*.

Merluzzo al Crudo
Roast cod fillets with tomatoes, basil and olive oil

Cod can be quite bland unless deep-fried, but prepared this way, roasted in a nutty polenta coating, it is very good. The coating came about one day by mistake – I ran out of flour and had to use polenta instead, which worked out so well that I decided to keep the recipe. When the singer Seal visited Zilli Fish recently, he ordered a roasted fish dish that included this cod. With this recipe, I love to serve a chilled Corvo Bianco from Sicily.

Serves 4
Preparation time: 10 minutes
Cooking time: 10 minutes

30ml (2 tablespoons) fine polenta flour
30ml (2 tablespoons) plain flour
salt and freshly ground black pepper
4 x 175–200g (6–7oz) pieces of cod fillet with skin on
30ml (2 tablespoons) vegetable oil

For the tomato and basil salsa
4–6 large plum tomatoes, skinned and seeded
1 red onion, peeled
1 garlic clove, peeled and crushed
grated zest and juice of 1 lime
125ml (4fl oz) olive oil
20 fresh basil leaves, torn into small pieces

- Pre-heat the oven to 240°C, 475°F, Gas Mark 9. Mix the polenta flour and plain flour on a large plate and season with salt and freshly ground black pepper. Coat the pieces of fish all over with the flour mixture, shaking off the excess.
- Heat the vegetable oil in an ovenproof frying pan. Add the fish and cook for 30 seconds on each side to sear. Transfer the pan to the oven and roast the fish for 7–9 minutes until just cooked.
- Meanwhile, make the salsa. Finely dice the tomatoes and onion and place in a bowl. Stir in the garlic, lime zest, lime juice and oil and season with salt and freshly ground black pepper.
- Transfer the fish to warmed serving plates. Mix the basil leaves into the salsa, then spoon over the fish to serve.

Fish

Salmone di Cremona
Salmon roasted with Italian mustard fruits

Mostarda di Cremona (mustard fruits) is a preserve of cherries, figs and pears in mustard and honey. It's easily found in all good Italian delis. Traditionally served with Bollito Misto (boiled meats), through experiments I found that it's delicious with fish too. Andros and Jackie love this dish, which is not surprising as the combination of flavours makes it a real winner.

Serves 4
Preparation time: 5 minutes
Cooking time: 10 minutes

4 x 200–225g (7–8oz) pieces of salmon fillet, preferably wild salmon
salt and freshly ground black pepper
20ml (4 teaspoons) vegetable oil
60ml (4 tablespoons) *mostarda di Cremona*, at room temperature

- Pre-heat the oven to 240°C, 475°F, Gas Mark 9. Season the pieces of salmon fillet with salt and freshly ground black pepper. Heat a non-stick frying pan, then add the oil. Put the salmon in the pan and sear on each side for 30 seconds.
- Transfer the fish to a baking tray, then roast for 6–8 minutes until the fish flakes but is still a little pink in the centre. Allow to rest for 2 minutes.
- Transfer the fish to warm plates and spoon over the *mostarda*.

Sgombro Ripieno
Mackerel stuffed with spinach and pine nuts

Ideally buy your fish from the fishmonger, so that all the hard work of cleaning and filleting the fish will be done for you, to perfection. 'Butterflied' simply means to bone a fish – removing the backbone, head and tail – keeping the two fillets attached . This recipe is also good using fresh sardines. I don't believe in wine 'rules' of red with meat and white with fish! This recipe is very well flavoured and filling, so I'd recommend a light red wine such as Bardolino or Valpolicella. Opt for a slightly more expensive one, as there is a good selection of these particular wines to choose from.

Serves 4
Preparation time: 10 minutes
Cooking time: 10 minutes

400g (14oz) spinach, washed and tough stalks removed
200g (7oz) pine nuts, toasted
salt and freshly ground black pepper
4 x 175g (6oz) mackerel, cleaned and butterflied
30ml (2 tablespoons) plain flour
2 eggs
30ml (2 tablespoons) chopped fresh flat-leaf parsley
40g (1½oz) unsalted butter
lemon wedges, to serve

- Bring a large pan of water to the boil. Add the spinach and cook for 1 minute until the leaves just wilt. Drain and squeeze out as much water as possible. Roughly chop the spinach and place in a bowl. Mix in the pine nuts and season with salt and freshly ground black pepper.
- Open out the fish flat, skin side down, and fill with the spinach mixture. Close up the fish again, enclosing the filling, and secure the opening with wooden cocktail sticks. Mix the flour with salt and freshly ground black pepper and use to dust the fish all over.
- Beat the eggs in a shallow bowl with the parsley. Heat a non-stick frying pan, then add the butter and heat until frothy. Dip the fish in the egg mixture to coat all over. Add the fish to the pan and cook for 3 minutes on each side until just beginning to brown. Drain on kitchen paper and serve with lemon wedges.

Spigola ai Peperoni
Herb-baked sea bass with roasted peppers

I think that this is one of the first fish recipes that I ever cooked, and it is still my family's favourite all these years later. This is also a favourite of my friends, and regular customers, Paul and Stacey Young. (You can see Stacey in the picture on the back cover of the book, enjoying some food I'd prepared for her and a few other friends.) Try this with a well-chilled Sauvignon del Friuli – a deliciously dry white with a hint of asparagus on the nose.

Serves 4
Preparation time: 10 minutes
Cooking time: 25–30 minutes

1 x 900g (2lb) sea bass, cleaned, head and tail removed and fish butterflied
3–4 fresh sage leaves
3–4 fresh basil leaves
4–5 fresh coriander leaves
1 sprig of fresh rosemary
1 garlic clove, peeled and crushed
45ml (3 tablespoons) vegetable oil
5ml (1 teaspoon) flaked sea salt
juice of ½ lemon
15ml (1 tablespoon) fine breadcrumbs
1 pepper (any colour)
lemon wedges, to serve

- Pre-heat the oven to 200°C, 400°F, Gas Mark 6. Open out the fish flat, skin side down. Place the sage, basil, coriander, rosemary and garlic along 1 fillet. Fold the other fillet over to cover the herbs. Using a sharp knife, make 2 diagonal slits in the skin.
- Heat the oil in a large ovenproof frying pan or a flameproof baking dish. Place the fish in the pan, slits side up, and cook for 2–3 minutes until the underside of the fish is golden brown. Sprinkle the salt and lemon juice over the fish and then the breadcrumbs. Cook for a further 2–3 minutes.
- Add the whole pepper to the pan and spoon over some of the juices. Place the pan in the oven and bake for 20 minutes until the fish is cooked through.
- Remove the pepper from the pan, peel off the skin and discard the seeds and core. Cut the pepper flesh into thin strips and sprinkle over the fish. Serve with lemon wedges.

Triglie alle Carbonara
Pan-roasted red mullet served with fettuccine carbonara

A combination of fish, meat and pasta might sound a bit over the top, but once tasted all together I'm sure you'll agree that it's great. The colours in this recipe are wonderful too. An alternative to filleting the red mullet is to roast the fish whole. When I cook this dish for my old friend, June Montana, I omit the fettuccine carbonara and just serve the fish with a crisp green salad. With anything creamy, I like to drink a slightly sparkling wine, such as a well-chilled Prosecco del Veneto.

Serves 2
Preparation time: 20 minutes
Cooking time: 8–12 minutes

2 x 225g (8oz) red mullets, filleted
30ml (2 tablespoons) plain flour
salt and freshly ground black pepper
25g (1oz) butter
juice of ½ lemon

For the sauce
15g (½oz) fresh basil leaves
50g (2oz) pine nuts
45ml (3 tablespoons) olive oil
5ml (1 teaspoon) flaked sea salt

For the fettuccine carbonara
15ml (1 tablespoon) sunflower oil
2 slices of Parma ham, chopped
3 egg yolks
30ml (2 tablespoons) double cream
30ml (2 tablespoons) freshly grated Parmesan cheese
175g (6oz) fettuccine (see page 214 for home-made fettuccine)

- Remove any remaining bones from the red mullet fillets. Place the flour on a plate and season well with salt and freshly ground black pepper. Coat the fish fillets all over with the seasoned flour. Set aside until required.
- To make the sauce, crush the basil leaves in a pestle and mortar. Add the pine nuts and

continue to pound and crush. Slowly drizzle in the oil, pounding in between additions to mix well. Mix in the salt flakes.

- To prepare the carbonara, heat the oil in a small pan, add the Parma ham and cook for 1–2 minutes until crisp. Drain on kitchen paper.
- In a large bowl, combine the egg yolks, cream and Parmesan cheese. Mix well and season with salt and freshly ground black pepper. Stir in the Parma ham.
- Bring a large pan of salted water to the boil. Add the fettuccine and cook for 5–8 minutes, or according to the instructions on the packet, until *al dente*.
- Meanwhile, heat the butter in a large frying pan. Add the fish and fry for 2–3 minutes on each side until golden brown and cooked through. Sprinkle with the lemon juice.
- Drain the pasta and immediately add to the egg and cream mixture. Toss for 2 minutes until the heat from the pasta lightly cooks the egg mixture. Arrange on a large warmed serving platter. Place the fish in the centre and spoon over the basil and pine nut sauce. Serve immediately.

Lombo di Tonno al Pepe Nero
Tuna fillet with black pepper

A great dish for a starter or main course, this is very popular in southern Italy, where the fish is eaten raw. If anyone in your party is not very keen on fish served rare, once sliced put the fish under the grill for a few more minutes. Leon Lenik, an old friend of mine, can regularly be found in my restaurants as, in his words, he loves all my food – including this dish, which deserves a strong, more up-market wine. I would recommend Gavi di Gavi.

Serves 4
Preparation time: 10 mintues
Cooking time: 5 minutes

1 x 350g (12oz) piece of fresh tuna fillet
30ml (2 tablespoons) black peppercorns, coarsely crushed in a pestle and mortar
450g (1lb) rocket
50g (2oz) Parmesan cheese, freshly grated
90ml (6 tablespoons) olive oil
juice of 2 lemons
15ml (1 tablespoon) flaked sea salt

- Pre-heat the oven to 220°C, 425°F, Gas Mark 7. Roll the tuna in the peppercorns to coat all over and place in a small roasting tin. Roast for 5 minutes; the tuna should still be pink in the centre.
- Meanwhile, arrange the rocket on a large serving plate.
- Thinly slice the tuna and arrange on the rocket. Sprinkle over the Parmesan cheese. Drizzle over the olive oil and lemon juice and, finally, sprinkle with the salt. Serve warm or cold.

Involtini di Pesce Spada con Penne e Broccoli
Rolled swordfish served with penne and broccoli

This is one of the first recipes I cooked on TV. My initial attempt was a complete disaster because we dropped it on the floor, but on the second, third and all subsequent shoots it worked particularly well and I was extremely pleased with the result. Sophie Grigson, this one is for you because I know it's one of your favourites.

Serves 4
Preparation time: 20 minutes
Cooking time: 20 minutes

75g (3oz) fresh white breadcrumbs
40g (1½oz) pecorino or Parmesan cheese, freshly grated
5 green celery leaves, chopped
salt and freshly ground black pepper
75ml (3fl oz) extra virgin olive oil
4 x 100g (4oz) thin slices of swordfish, thawed if frozen
1 sprig of fresh rosemary
300g (11oz) penne pasta
450g (1lb) broccoli, trimmed and divided into small florets
1 garlic clove, peeled and crushed
2 fresh red chillies, seeded and diagonally sliced
grated zest of 1 lemon
celery leaves, to garnish

- Pre-heat the oven to 200°C, 400°F, Gas Mark 6. In a large bowl, mix together the breadcrumbs, 25g (1oz) of the cheese, the celery leaves, a little salt and 15ml (1 tablespoon) of the oil to form a paste.
- Place the slices of fish between sheets of cling film and pound with a rolling pin to flatten slightly. Remove the film. Divide the crumb and cheese paste equally among the slices of fish, spreading it out evenly. Roll up the fish and secure each roll with a wooden cocktail stick.
- Place the fish rolls on a baking tray and drizzle with 15ml (1 tablespoon) olive oil. Add the rosemary sprig. Roast for 10 minutes.
- Meanwhile, cook the pasta in a large pan of boiling salted water for 10–12 minutes, or according to the instructions on the packet, until *al dente*; drain. At the same time, cook

the broccoli in a pan of simmering water for 5 minutes until tender and bright green; drain and refresh.

- Heat the remaining 45ml (3 tablespoons) olive oil in large frying pan and add the garlic and chillies. Cook for 1 minute, then add the broccoli and lemon zest. Cook for 3–4 minutes, stirring frequently. Stir in the pasta and the remaining cheese. Season well with salt and freshly ground black pepper to taste, then transfer to a large warmed serving dish.
- Diagonally slice each fish roll and place on the pasta. Garnish with fresh celery leaves to serve.

Totani Ripieni in Casseruola
Braised stuffed squid with pork sausage

I was inspired to make this recipe six years ago in Portugal and it has been a success ever since. I believe that mixing fish and meat really does work with Mediterranean cooking.

Serves 4
Preparation time: 45 minutes plus soaking
Cooking time: 1 hour 45 minutes

75g (3oz) dried cannellini beans, soaked overnight
4 medium squid, skinned and cleaned
175g (6oz) pork sausagemeat
2 medium potatoes, about 275g (10oz), peeled and diced
1 large onion, peeled and sliced
10 plum tomatoes, skinned, seeded and diced
1 fennel bulb, trimmed and thinly sliced
2 garlic cloves, peeled and finely chopped
1 fresh red chilli, seeded and finely chopped
30ml (2 tablespoons) salted capers, rinsed
1 bay leaf
300ml (10fl oz) red wine
1.2 litres (2 pints) chicken stock
90ml (6 tablespoons) extra virgin olive oil
salt and freshly ground black pepper
45ml (3 tablespoons) chopped fresh flat-leaf parsley
10 fresh basil leaves, roughly torn

- Drain the beans, place in a saucepan and cover with fresh cold water. Bring to the boil and simmer for 25 minutes. Drain.
- Pre-heat the oven to 180°C, 350°F, Gas Mark 4. Slit open the squid bodies down one side and open out flat. Using a sharp knife, score the inner side of each body with diagonal lines about 1cm (½in) apart. Give the squid a quarter turn and score again to make a criss-cross pattern.
- Turn the squid over, criss-cross side down. Divide the sausage meat among the squid, placing it in a line down the centre. Roll up the squid and secure each with a wooden cocktail stick.
- Place the potatoes, beans and onion in a casserole dish and mix in the tomatoes, fennel, garlic, chilli, capers, bay leaf, red wine and stock. Place the stuffed squid and the squid tentacles on top. Drizzle over 60ml (4 tablespoons) of the oil and season with salt and

freshly ground black pepper. Cover tightly and bake for 1 hour 20 minutes, spooning some of the cooking juices over the squid occasionally.

- The squid should be very tender at the end of the cooking. Stir the parsley and basil leaves into the casserole and drizzle with the remaining oil to serve.

Cotolette di Maiale Ripiene
Pork chops stuffed with smoked mozzarella and sage

This recipe is very easy to prepare and would make a good Christmas alternative to turkey. If the meat seems to be a little dry, make a gravy by dissolving a meat stock cube in some water and adding a few drops of balsamic vinegar.

Serves 4
Preparation time: 15 minutes
Cooking time: 40 minutes

60ml (4 tablespoons) olive oil
225g (8oz) button mushrooms, thinly sliced
salt and freshly ground black pepper
4 x 175g (6oz) pork loin chops, cut 1cm (½in) thick
1 x 125g (5oz) smoked mozzarella cheese, diced
75g (3oz) butter
150ml (5fl oz) dry white wine
2 fresh sage leaves
Spinaci all'Aglio, Olio e Peperoncino (see page 131), to serve

- Pre-heat the oven to 190°C, 375°F, Gas Mark 5. Heat 30ml (2 tablespoons) of the oil in a frying pan, add the mushrooms and sauté for 3 minutes until golden brown. Season with salt and freshly ground black pepper.
- Using a very sharp knife, cut a pocket horizontally in each pork chop. Mix the mozzarella with the mushrooms, then spoon into the chops. Press them back into shape and secure the opening with a skewer or wooden cocktail sticks.
- Heat the remaining 30ml (2 tablespoons) of the oil in a large ovenproof frying pan. Add the stuffed pork chops and cook for 3 minutes on each side until golden brown. Transfer the pan to the oven to cook for a further 25 minutes.
- Meanwhile, place the butter, wine, sage and freshly ground black pepper to taste in a small saucepan. Simmer for 5 minutes.
- Divide the hot spinach among 4 warmed serving plates. Add a pork chop to each plate, spoon the sauce over the top and serve immediately.

Suprema di Pollo Ripieno
Stuffed chicken supremes with Parma ham and Parmesan cheese

This recipe is perfect for a working couple with children – with little time to cook, they will still want tasty and healthy meals, and this just fits the bill. I cooked this when filming the flying episode for The Italian Job. *My friends, Nigel and Mandy, are fans of this dish.*

Serves 4
Preparation time: 15 minutes
Cooking time: 25 minutes

100g (4oz) butter, softened
60ml (4 tablespoons) freshly grated Parmesan cheese
4 x 175g (6oz) chicken supremes (breasts on the bone), skinned and wing bone trimmed
4 thin slices of Parma ham
4 fresh sage leaves

- Pre-heat the oven to 200°C, 400°F, Gas Mark 6. Mix three-quarters of the butter with the Parmesan cheese; chill in the freezer until required.
- Remove the fillet from each chicken supreme. Place the fillets between sheets of cling film and pound with a rolling pin to flatten. Cut a pocket horizontally in each chicken supreme, cutting about half-way through.
- Divide the chilled butter into 4 equal portions and shape each into a sausage shape. Put a portion of the butter in the incision cut in the chicken supreme, then cover with a flattened fillet. Place a slice of Parma ham on a flat surface and put a sage leaf in the centre; set a chicken supreme on the sage leaf and roll the Parma ham around the chicken. Secure with a wooden cocktail stick. Repeat with the remaining chicken, butter filling, Parma ham and sage leaves.
- Melt the remaining butter in an ovenproof frying pan. Add the chicken and cook for 5 minutes until browned all over. Transfer the pan to the oven and roast for 20 minutes until the chicken is tender. The juices should run clear when the chicken is pierced with the point of a sharp knife. Serve immediately with the cooking juices spooned over the top.

Stinco alle Albicocche
Pork knuckle slow-roasted with herbs and apricots

Despite its rather unfortunate-sounding Italian name, this is a dish that tastes and looks great. Although extremely time-consuming to prepare, it is still well worth the effort. The herbs and apricots give a wonderful flavour. Serve with a good Chianti, opened well in advance of serving.

Serves 4
Preparation time: 30 minutes plus soaking
Cooking time: 4 hours

2 x 700g (1½lb) pork knuckles
25g (1oz) unsalted butter
1 medium onion, peeled and chopped
2 garlic cloves, peeled and chopped
45ml (3 tablespoons) chopped fresh sage leaves
2 sprigs of fresh rosemary, stalks discarded and leaves finely chopped
250g (9oz) no-soak dried apricots
creamy mashed potatoes, to serve (optional)
30ml (2 tablespoons) chopped fresh flat-leaf parsley

- Place the knuckles in a large pan and cover with cold water. Bring to the boil, skimming the surface of any scum. Reduce the heat and simmer for 2 hours until the meat is tender.
- Remove the knuckles from the cooking liquid. Continue to boil the liquid until reduced by half. Meanwhile, remove the fat and sinew from the knuckles and split each in half lengthways, leaving the bone in each half.
- Melt the butter in a saucepan, add the onion, garlic, sage and rosemary, and fry for 5 minutes until golden brown. Stir in the apricots and reduced cooking liquid. Simmer for 30 minutes until the sauce is thick and syrupy.
- Pre-heat the oven to 200°C, 400°F, Gas Mark 6.
- Place the split pork knuckles in a casserole dish and pour over the apricot sauce. Cover and roast for 45 minutes, basting the knuckles with the sauce at least once.
- Arrange the knuckles on warm serving plates with creamy mashed potato, if using. Spoon over the apricot sauce and sprinkle with the chopped parsley to serve.

Spaghetti all'Astice (page 27)

Involtini di Pesce Spada con Penne e Broccoli (page 66)

Cotolette di Maiale Ripiene (page 70)

Bufala, Ruchetta e Peperoni (page 44)

Tacchino Canzanese
Herbed turkey escalopes with fresh lime

Canzano is the village in the Abruzzo region where my mother was born, and I have given the dish its title because the recipe is one I remember from my childhood. These turkey escalopes make an excellent summer meal served with steamed new potatoes and a simple salad of fresh tomatoes, finely chopped onions, basil and rocket.

Serves 4
Preparation time: 15 minutes
Cooking time: 10 minutes

4 x 225g (8oz) turkey escalopes
salt and freshly ground black pepper
1 sprig of fresh rosemary, stalk discarded and leaves finely chopped
100g (4oz) plain flour
2 eggs
100g (4oz) dried breadcrumbs
45ml (3 tablespoons) sunflower oil
50g (2oz) Parmesan cheese, freshly grated
1 lime, quartered

- Season each turkey escalope with salt and freshly ground black pepper. Sprinkle with the chopped rosemary.
- Place the flour on a large plate; beat the eggs on another plate and spread the breadcrumbs on a third plate. First coat each escalope in flour, then egg and, finally, coat with breadcrumbs, pressing the crumbs well onto the escalopes.
- Preheat the grill to medium-hot. Heat half of the oil in a large frying pan and add 2 escalopes. Fry for 2 minutes on each side until golden brown. Transfer to a foil-lined grill pan. Repeat with remaining oil and escalopes.
- Sprinkle the escalopes with the Parmesan cheese and grill for 1–2 minutes until the cheese is melted and bubbling. Serve the escalopes immediately with the lime wedges.

Poultry and White Meats

Galletto al Forno
Roasted spring chickens

In Italy, spring chickens are normally cooked on a spit. For this recipe, the birds are split in half and roasted, although the cooking can also be done on a barbecue. Make sure that each chicken half has its seasoning of rosemary, garlic and chilli. When I barbecue, I love drinking chilled Italian beer such as Peroni.

Serves 4
Preparation time: 10 minutes
Cooking time: 35 minutes

4 spring chickens
flaked sea salt and freshly ground black pepper
100ml (4fl oz) olive oil
4 garlic cloves, crushed in their skins
4 sprigs of fresh rosemary
2 fresh red chillies, seeded and roughly chopped (optional)
150ml (5fl oz) dry white wine
150ml (5fl oz) hot chicken stock

- Pre-heat the oven to 200°C, 400°F, Gas Mark 6. Place the spring chickens on a chopping board and, using a strong-bladed sharp knife, halve each bird lengthways. Rub the chicken halves with salt and freshly ground black pepper.
- Place all the chicken halves in a large roasting tin, skin side down, and drizzle over the oil. Add the garlic, rosemary and chillies, if using. Roast for 5 minutes.
- Turn the chicken halves over and add the wine and stock to the roasting tin. Return to the oven and roast for a further 30 minutes until the chickens are golden brown and cooked through. Serve immediately with some of the cooking juices spooned over the top.

Filetto al Dolcelatte
Pork fillet wrapped with courgettes and melting dolcelatte

Fillet, or tenderloin, is a very tender cut of pork that is easy and quick to cook. It's great served with simple sauces like butter and sage. One of my longest-serving chefs, Giuseppe, and I came up with this recipe one day many years ago, and it has been a winner on the menu ever since. A dry white wine such as Pinot Grigio is perfect with pork cooked this way.

Serves 4
Preparation time: 20 minutes plus standing
Cooking time: 15 minutes

2 large courgettes, about 450g (1lb) in total
salt and freshly ground black pepper
60ml (4 tablespoons) olive oil
4 x 200g (7oz) pieces of pork fillet
200g (7oz) dolcelatte cheese, thinly sliced

- Using a potato peeler, slice the courgettes lengthways into ribbons. Sprinkle with a little salt and leave to drain in a colander for 20 minutes. Rinse with cold water, then pat dry on kitchen paper.
- Pre-heat a griddle until smoking hot. Add some of the oil and heat. Spread half of the courgette ribbons on the griddle and cook for 1–2 minutes on each side. Remove and cook the remaining courgette ribbons. Keep to one side.
- Season the meat with salt and freshly ground black pepper, then sear all over on the hot griddle, adding extra oil if necessary. Remove.
- Pre-heat the grill to medium-hot. Wrap the pieces of pork with the courgette ribbons and place on a foil-lined grill pan. Top with the slices of dolcelatte. Grill for 4–5 minutes until the cheese is melted and bubbling and the meat is cooked through. Serve immediately.

Costolette al Burro e Salvia
Pork chops in sage butter

This recipe calls for French-trimmed pork chops, which means that they have had all the fat and gristle removed from the ends of the chop bones (as is often done with lamb cutlets), making a better appearance. You could add some halved open cap mushrooms, cooking them in the sage butter, if you like.

Serves 4
Preparation time: 10 minutes
Cooking time: 20 minutes

4 x 200g (7oz) French-trimmed pork chops
salt and freshly ground black pepper
60ml (4 tablespoons) dry white wine
100g (4oz) unsalted butter
20 fresh sage leaves
juice of ½ lemon

- Pre-heat the grill to medium-hot. Season the pork chops all over with salt and freshly ground black pepper. Place the chops in a large ovenproof frying pan and place under the grill. Cook the chops for 7 minutes on each side until golden brown and tender. Transfer the chops to a warmed serving plate and keep warm.
- Place the frying pan on the hob and add the wine. Bring to the boil, stirring to mix with the cooking juices; boil to reduce by half. Add the butter to the pan with the sage leaves and lemon juice. Cook for 1–2 minutes, stirring constantly, until the sauce is frothy. Pour the sauce over the chops and serve immediately.

Petto di Pollo Orientale
Chicken breasts with pineapple and bok choy

People often ask me if I cook anything other than Italian food at home, and my answer is that Chinese food is one of my favourites. It's probably because I've worked in Soho for so many years, and this has inspired me to use oriental herbs, spices and vegetables in my kitchen. I devised this recipe whilst experimenting at home, and dedicate it to all my Chinese neighbours in Soho. You will need 8 bamboo (or wooden) skewers which must be soaked in cold water beforehand to prevent them from burning.

Serves 4
Preparation time: 20 minutes
Cooking time: 15–20 minutes

60ml (4 tablespoons) dark soy sauce
15ml (1 tablespoon) finely chopped fresh root ginger
30ml (2 tablespoons) chopped fresh coriander
15ml (1 tablespoon) clear honey
juice of 1 orange
4 x 175g (6oz) boneless chicken breasts, each cut into 6 pieces
salt and freshly ground black pepper
1 medium-size pineapple, peeled, cored and cut into large chunks
45ml (3 tablespoons) sunflower oil
5ml (1 teaspoon) toasted sesame oil
450g (1lb) baby bok choy, shredded
45ml (3 tablespoons) oyster sauce

- Place the soy sauce in a large bowl and mix in the ginger, coriander, honey and orange juice. Add the chicken pieces and mix well to coat.
- Rub the soaked bamboo skewers with salt and freshly ground black pepper (this is a good way of seasoning the meat throughout). Thread the chicken and pineapple chunks on to the skewers. Reserve the soy sauce mixture.
- Heat a griddle on the hob until almost smoking. Add some of the oil and heat. Place the skewers on the griddle and cook for 8–10 minutes, turning frequently and brushing with the soy sauce mixture.
- Meanwhile, heat a large wok or heavy-based frying pan until smoking hot. Add the remaining sunflower oil with the sesame oil and heat. Add the shredded bok choy and stir-fry for 3–5 minutes. Add the oyster sauce and stir-fry for a further 2 minutes.
- Divide the bok choy among 4 warmed serving plates and place 2 skewers on each. Serve immediately.

Voldostana di Pollo alle Mandorle
Deep-fried chicken breasts stuffed with fontina and ricotta cheeses

These chicken breasts are delicious served with a pasta such as Spaghetti alla Crudaiola (see page 20) or a crisp mixed salad. I particularly like this dish because of the toasted almonds – they give a lovely texture and flavour.

Serves 4
Preparation time: 20 minutes
Cooking time: 5–8 minutes

4 x 200g (7oz) boneless chicken breasts, skinned
75g (3oz) fontina or Gruyère cheese, grated
75g (3oz) ricotta cheese
50g (2oz) cooked ham, finely chopped
salt and freshly ground black pepper
50g (2oz) plain flour
2 eggs
50g (2oz) ground almonds
50g (2oz) dried breadcrumbs
sunflower oil for deep-frying

To serve
2 heads of chicory
1 pink grapefruit, segmented
150g (5oz) seedless white grapes
juice of 1 lemon
60ml (4 tablespoons) olive oil
40g (1½oz) flaked almonds, toasted

- Split the chicken breasts in half horizontally, open out like a book and place between sheets of cling film. Pound with a rolling pin to flatten.
- Place the fontina and ricotta cheeses in a bowl and mix in the ham. Season with salt and freshly ground black pepper. Divide the mixture evenly among the chicken breasts, spooning it into the centre. Fold the chicken to enclose the stuffing and secure with wooden cocktail sticks.
- Place the flour on a plate and season with salt and freshly ground black pepper. Beat the eggs on another plate. Mix the ground almonds and breadcrumbs on a third plate. First

coat the chicken with flour, then with egg and, finally, with the almond mixture.

- Heat enough oil in a large pan to deep-fry. The oil is hot enough when it reaches 160°C, 325°F or when a piece of bread dropped into the oil will sizzle and turn golden brown in 30 seconds. Gently place the chicken breasts in the oil, cooking them 2 at a time, and deep-fry for 5–8 minutes, turning at least once, until golden brown all over. The chicken should be cooked through and not at all pink. Drain on kitchen paper.
- Meanwhile, arrange the chicory leaves on 4 large serving plates and randomly place the grapefruit and grapes on top.
- Diagonally slice each chicken breast and place in the centre of each plate. Drizzle with the lemon juice and olive oil. Sprinkle over the flaked almonds and serve.

Pollo ai Peperoni
Sliced chicken supremes with sweet peppers

You could try this with a plain risotto with Parmesan cheese (see page 218) or wet polenta (see page 217) – both would be excellent accompaniments. The sauce is quite spicy, so if serving to children, I suggest you omit the chilli.

Serves 4
Preparation time: 20 minutes
Cooking times: 40 minutes

30ml (2 tablespoons) olive oil
3 large peppers (1 yellow, 1 red and 1 orange), cored, seeded and cut into strips
1 fresh red chilli, seeded and chopped
4 chicken supremes (breasts on the bone), sliced into long thick strips
150ml (5fl oz) dry white wine
1 garlic clove, peeled and chopped
600g (1¼lb) tomatoes, skinned and chopped
salt and freshly ground black pepper

- Heat the oil in a large frying pan, add the peppers and fry for 5–8 minutes until just soft. Add the chilli and the strips of chicken and cook for a further 5 minutes, stirring occasionally.
- Add the wine and cook for 5 minutes until most of the liquid has evaporated.
- Stir in the garlic and tomatoes and season with salt and freshly ground black pepper. Cook over a low heat for 20 minutes. Serve hot.

Tiramisù del Boscaiolo
Fruits of the forest tiramisù

This recipe was created in the restaurant by chance. One day the fruit and vegetable man got the order mixed up and delivered too many berries. Not wanting to waste them, I looked around my kitchen for inspiration. A tiramisù *was being made at the time, and so this dish was created. It's been a great success ever since, especially with my friend Neil Reading.*

Serves 6
Preparation time: 30 minutes plus chilling

600ml (1 pint) double cream
250g (9oz) mascarpone cheese
120ml (8 tablespoons) caster sugar
6 egg yolks
1.2 litres (2 pints) hot strong black coffee
15ml (1 tablespoon) Marsala wine
15ml (1 tablespoon) Tia Maria liqueur
450g (1lb) Savoiardi biscuits
450g (1lb) fresh fruits of the forest, such as raspberries, strawberries, redcurrants and
    blackberries, wiped clean, stalks removed and sliced if necessary

- Place the cream in a bowl with the mascarpone cheese and 60ml (4 tablespoons) of the caster sugar. Whisk well until the sugar dissolves and the cream is just thick.
- In another bowl whisk the egg yolks with the remaining sugar for about 10 minutes until the mixture is quite thick, light and fluffy. Using a large metal spoon, fold the egg yolk mixture into the mascarpone mixture.
- Mix together the coffee, Marsala and Tia Maria in a shallow bowl.
- To assemble the tiramisù, spoon one-third of the mascarpone mixture into the bottom of a 1.8 litre (3 pint) dish that is 7.5cm (3in) deep. Taking one biscuit at a time, dip half of the biscuits into the coffee mixture and arrange in a single layer on the mascarpone. Top with half of the fruits. Spoon another one-third of the mascarpone mixture over the fruit and cover with the remaining biscuits moistened with the coffee mixture. Spread the remaining mascarpone mixture on the top and finish with the remaining fruits, arranged decoratively.
- Cover the tiramisù with cling film and chill for at least 6 hours in the refrigerator to set slightly. Serve chilled.

Panna Cotta al Cioccolato
Vanilla mousse with dark chocolate sauce

This is extremely light, especially if you skip the chocolate sauce or serve the panna cotta *with a fresh fruit coulis. Strictly speaking, it isn't a mousse, but that sounds more appealing than the direct English translation of* panna cotta, *which is 'cooked cream'. If you prefer, use agar agar rather than gelatine to set the mousse.*

Serves 6
Preparation time: 30 minutes plus chilling
Cooking time: 20 minutes

3 gelatine leaves or 1 tablespoon powdered gelatine
300ml (10fl oz) double cream
300ml (10fl oz) milk
100g (4oz) caster sugar
6 drops of vanilla essence

For the chocolate curls
100g (4oz) good-quality plain chocolate, chopped

For the chocolate sauce
100g (4oz) good-quality plain chocolate, chopped
125ml (4fl oz) water
50g (2oz) caster sugar
25g (1oz) butter

- If using gelatine leaves, soak in a little cold water to soften, then drain. If using powdered gelatine, soften in 45–60ml (3–4 tablespoons) warm water.
- Meanwhile, place the cream in a saucepan with the milk and sugar. Heat gently until the sugar dissolves, stirring frequently. Bring to just below boiling point. Away from the heat, stir the gelatine into the cream mixture until dissolved, then add the vanilla essence. Pour the cream mixture into 6 x 150ml (5fl oz) ramekins. Allow to cool, then chill for 1 hour until set.
- Meanwhile, melt the chocolate for the curls in a heatproof bowl set over a pan of simmering water. Once melted, remove the bowl from the pan and beat the chocolate with a plastic spatula until cooled – this will make the chocolate quite glossy. Thinly spread the chocolate on a cold surface and leave to set (do not chill in the refrigerator). Using a palette knife, slide the edge along the chocolate to make curls. Keep the curls in a cool place (not the refrigerator).

- For the chocolate sauce, place all the ingredients in a heatproof bowl set over a pan of simmering water and heat gently until the chocolate melts and the sugar dissolves, stirring frequently to blend the sauce together. Cover with cling film and allow to cool, stirring occasionally.
- To assemble, spoon the chocolate sauce on to 6 serving plates. Dip the base of each ramekin in a bowl of hot water to loosen the *panna cotta*, then turn out on to the chocolate sauce. Top with chocolate curls and serve.

Desserts

Tagliolini al Gelato
Pancake tagliolini with white chocolate ice cream and raspberry coulis

An impressive dessert. The term 'tagliolini' is normally applied to pasta, but I've used the word here because the sliced pancakes do look like long thin pasta. The last time I had lunch with the Women's Editor of the Sun, *Jane Moore, she skipped a starter so she could enjoy this marvellous dessert.*

Serves 4
Preparation time: 20 minutes
Cooking time: 20–30 minutes

1 egg
150ml (5fl oz) milk
15ml (1 tablespoon) sunflower oil
65g (2½oz) plain flour
scoops of white chocolate or vanilla ice cream, to serve

For the coulis
450g (1lb) fresh or frozen raspberries
60ml (4 tablespoons) brown sugar

For the sauce
60ml (4 tablespoons) caster sugar
15g (½oz) butter
200ml (7fl oz) fresh orange juice

- For the pancakes, mix the egg, milk and half of the oil in a jug. Sift the flour into a bowl and gradually beat in the egg mixture to make a smooth batter. Heat an 18cm (7in) frying pan. Using a piece of kitchen paper, wipe some of the remaining oil over the bottom of the pan. Pour one-quarter of the batter into the pan, swirling round to spread the batter evenly. Cook for 1–2 minutes until the pancake is set and golden on the base. Flip over and cook for a further 1–2 minutes until golden on the other side. Place the pancake on greaseproof paper. Make another 3 pancakes in the same way, oiling the pan as necessary.
- Thinly slice the pancakes into strips. Set aside.
- For the coulis, place the raspberries in a saucepan with the brown sugar and simmer for 5 minutes, stirring occasionally, until the raspberries break up to make a sauce. Press through a sieve to make a purée, and allow to cool.

- Meanwhile, place the caster sugar, butter and orange juice in a frying pan and heat gently, stirring, until the sugar dissolves. Bring to the boil and boil for 3–4 minutes until quite syrupy. Add the strips of pancake and stir into the sauce; cook for 1 minute.
- To serve, spoon the raspberry coulis on to 4 chilled serving plates and top with scoops of ice cream. Spoon the pancake tagliolini over the ice cream. Serve immediately.

Zabaione al Marsala
Traditional zabaione served with strawberries

This dessert must be served warm, as soon as it is ready. Don't worry if it takes a few attempts to get the recipe right – practice makes perfect and it is definitely worth it! For the best results, use a round copper pan.

Serves 6
Preparation time: 20 minutes
Cooking time: 15 minutes

4 egg yolks
65g (2½oz) caster sugar
125ml (4fl oz) sweet Marsala wine
100g (4oz) fresh strawberries
8 Savoiardi biscuits or sponge fingers, to serve

- Place the egg yolks and sugar in a large heatproof bowl. Whisk until the sugar dissolves, then add the Marsala and whisk to mix.
- Set the bowl over a pan of simmering water and whisk for about 15 minutes until the mixture is very thick and creamy.
- Quickly pour the *zabaione* into 6 tall glasses and serve immediately, with the strawberries and biscuits.

Misto di Frutta alla Vaniglia
Sautéed figs, peaches and apricots with vanilla

There is nothing like a perfectly ripe, fresh fig! We used to have a fig tree in our front garden, and as children we would eat the fruit until it came out of our ears. For this recipe you can use a combination of whichever fruits are in season. For example, in winter you might want to try a mixture of tropical varieties such as mango and papaya or traditional apples and pears.

Serves 4
Preparation time: 15 minutes
Cooking time: 5–8 minutes

4 peaches, stoned and each sliced into 8
4 apricots, stoned and quartered
4 figs, quartered
100g (4oz) caster sugar
3 drops of vanilla essence
50g (2oz) unsalted butter
200g (7oz) crème fraîche

- Bring a saucepan of water to the boil. Add all the fruit and blanch for 1–2 minutes. Drain, reserving both the fruit and the liquid. Cool the fruit and then remove the skins.
- Place 150ml (5fl oz) of the reserved fruit liquid in a saucepan and add the caster sugar and vanilla essence. Heat gently to dissolve the sugar, then bring to the boil. Boil for 3 minutes until syrupy.
- Melt the butter in a large frying pan, add the peaches and apricots and sauté for 30 seconds. Add the figs and sauté for another 30 seconds. Add the syrup and bring to the boil.
- Serve immediately, with the crème fraîche spooned over the fruit.

Pizzetta alla Banana
Sweet pizza with rum bananas

Pizza is normally savoury, but with the addition of a little sugar it can also work well as a crusty dessert base. For children, just omit the rum. This sweet pizza is a favourite with my Bananarama friends, Karen and Sarah.

Serves 6
Preparation time: 30 minutes plus proving
Cooking time: 10–15 minutes

250g (9oz) strong white bread flour
pinch of salt
30ml (2 tablespoons) caster sugar
10ml (2 teaspoons) easy-blend dried yeast
30ml (2 tablespoons) warm water
2 large eggs, beaten
100g (4oz) unsalted butter, cut into cubes and softened

For the topping
50g (2oz) unsalted butter
100g (4oz) caster sugar
pinch of freshly grated nutmeg
5ml (1 teaspoon) ground cinnamon
6 ripe bananas, peeled and roughly chopped
30ml (2 tablespoons) dark rum

- Sift the flour and salt into a large mixing bowl. Stir in the sugar and yeast. Make a well in the centre. Add the water, eggs and butter to the well and gradually beat into the dry ingredients with a wooden spoon to form a rough dough. Turn out onto a floured surface and knead for 5 minutes until the dough is smooth and firm. Place in a clean floured bowl and cover with cling film. Leave in a warm place for 1 hour until well risen.
- Pre-heat the oven to 180°C, 350°F, Gas Mark 4. Knead the dough again briefly to knock out the air, then divide into 6 portions. Roll out each portion of dough to a round 15–20cm (6–8in) in diameter and place on a baking sheet. Bake for 7 minutes until risen and golden.
- Meanwhile, make the topping. Place the butter in a frying pan with the sugar and spices. Cook over a low heat until the sugar dissolves. Add the bananas and bring the mixture to the boil. Add the rum and ignite to flambé the bananas. Once the flames have died down, simmer for 3–4 minutes until the bananas are tender.
- Spoon the bananas over the sweet pizza bases. Serve warm.

Semifreddo allo Yoghurt e Rabarbaro
Iced yoghurt and walnut timbales with rhubarb sauce

An excellent dessert for a barbecue on a very hot day. This is one of the few desserts I prepare at home when entertaining guests in the summer.

Serves 6
Preparation time: 15 minutes
Cooking time: 5 minutes

450g (1lb) plain yoghurt
75g (3oz) icing sugar, sifted
juice of 1 lemon
100g (4oz) walnuts, toasted and chopped

For the praline
100g (4oz) granulated sugar
75ml (3fl oz) water
75g (3oz) walnuts, toasted and roughly chopped

For the sauce
1 x 539g (18oz) can rhubarb, drained
100g (4oz) icing sugar

- Line 6 x 150ml (5fl oz) ramekins with cling film. Place the yoghurt in a bowl and stir in the icing sugar, lemon juice and walnuts. Spoon into the prepared ramekins. Freeze for 2–3 hours until just set.
- For the praline, place the granulated sugar and water in a saucepan and heat gently to dissolve the sugar. Bring to the boil and boil for 3–5 minutes until the syrup turns a golden brown caramel colour. Stir in the walnuts. Spoon on to a greased baking sheet and leave to cool. When set, crush the walnut praline.
- For the sauce, process the rhubarb in a food processor with the icing sugar.
- Remove the yoghurt timbales from the freezer about 20 minutes before required and allow to stand at room temperature. Then turn out on to serving plates. Spoon some of the rhubarb sauce round the timbales and sprinkle with the walnut praline to serve.

Frutta al Mascarpone
Mascarpone with individual fruit cakes

This is perfect for all the family, and because it can be kept in the refrigerator for a few days it's great for unexpected guests.

Serves 4
Preparation time: 10 minutes
Cooking time: 10–12 minutes

50g (2oz) unsalted butter, softened
50g (2oz) caster sugar
1 egg
75g (3oz) plain flour
2.5ml (½ teaspoon) baking powder
100g (4oz) mixed dried fruit, soaked in 45ml (3 tablespoons) brandy
grated zest of ½ lemon
90ml (6 tablespoons) mascarpone cheese

- Pre-heat the oven to 180°C, 350°F, Gas Mark 4. Place a baking sheet in the oven to heat. Grease 4 x 150ml (5fl oz) ramekins and line the bottoms with greased greaseproof paper.
- Place the butter in a large bowl and cream with the caster sugar until light and fluffy. Gradually beat in the egg.
- Sift the flour and baking powder into a bowl and and stir in the soaked fruits and lemon zest. Gradually beat the flour mixture into the egg mixture.
- Spoon the cake mixture into the prepared ramekins and level the surface. Place on the hot baking sheet in the oven and bake for 10–12 minutes until well risen and firm to the touch.
- Allow to cool for 5 minutes, then turn out the cakes and serve warm with the mascarpone cheese. The mascarpone should melt over the warm cakes.

Gelato alla Fragola
Strawberry ice cream

Italians are well known for the variety and excellence of their ice creams. The recipe here is extremely quick to make, and simply delicious. Feel free to substitute other seasonal fruit for the strawberries.

Serves 4–6
Preparation time: 20 minutes plus freezing
Cooking time: 5–8 minutes

600ml (1 pint) double cream
150ml (5fl oz) milk
100g (4oz) caster sugar
5 egg yolks
225g (8oz) strawberries, wiped clean and hulled

- Place the cream in a heavy-based saucepan with the milk and sugar. Heat gently until the sugar dissolves, stirring occasionally, then bring to just below boiling point.
- Place the egg yolks in a bowl and whisk together, at the same time pouring in the warm cream mixture. Wipe the saucepan clean, then return the cream mixture to the pan. Over a very gentle heat, cook the custard for 3–5 minutes, stirring constantly, until thickened enough to coat the spoon. Do not allow the custard to boil or it will curdle. Once thick, immediately pour the custard into a clean bowl.
- Place the strawberries in a food processor and process until smooth. Pour the strawberry purée into the custard and stir to mix. Set the bowl over another bowl filled with ice and stir the mixture until cold.
- Transfer the mixture to a deep plastic container and freeze for 2–3 hours until just set.
- Turn the just frozen mixture into a bowl and mash with a fork. Return to the plastic container and freeze for a further 3 hours until set.
- Remove from the freezer about 20 minutes before required to bring to room temperature before serving.

Pesche al Vino Rosso
Peaches in red wine and cinnamon

This is a simple but effective dessert. If you are very pushed for time, simply chop up the peaches, add to the strained wine syrup and chill. A light red wine, such as Valpolicella would be a good choice for poaching the peaches

Serves 4
Preparation time: 10 minutes
Cooking time: 20–25 minutes

1 x 75cl bottle red wine
juice of 1 orange, strained
juice of ½ lemon, strained
250ml (9fl oz) water
250g (9oz) caster sugar
2.5ml (½ teaspoon) vanilla essence
1 cinnamon stick, halved
1 bay leaf
8 small peaches

- Place the wine in a large pan and stir in the orange and lemon juices, water, sugar, vanilla essence, cinnamon stick and bay leaf. Heat gently to dissolve the sugar, stirring occasionally, then bring to the boil. Simmer for 10 minutes.
- Add the peaches to the wine mixture and cover with damp greaseproof paper (the paper should touch the fruit and liquid). Simmer for 10–15 minutes until the peaches are soft. Remove from heat and allow to cool.
- Remove the peaches with a slotted spoon and peel off the skins. Place the peaches in a large bowl. Strain the syrup over the fruit, discarding the cinnamon and bay leaf. Chill before serving.

Easter

Easter is an important occasion in the Italian calendar and widely celebrated with friends and family, whereas Christmas is considered to be very much a family occasion. Each region has its own special dishes for Easter. However, there will always be lamb and wheat on the menu, all across Italy.

As a small child, I cherished Easter Monday, or *Pasquetta*; my brothers, sister and I would go for brilliant picnics, taking with us all the left-over food from the feast the day before. This was great from my mother's point of view as all the food would be eaten and she'd have a few hours of peace and quiet!

Rollatini di Scamorza al Prosciutto con Pera e Radicchio

Smoked mozzarella wrapped in Parma ham, with pear and radicchio

This has to be my all-time favourite. It's a brilliant starter and also great for party nibbles. The dish was served at my wedding in Abruzzo, and everyone loved it when we barbecued on the beach.

Serves 8
Preparation time: 10 minutes
Cooking time: 15 minutes

4 firm, yet ripe pears
60ml (4 tablespoons) caster sugar
600ml (1 pint) water
2 x 125g (5oz) smoked mozzarella cheeses
8 slices of Parma ham, each cut into 3 pieces
25g (1oz) butter
30ml (2 tablespoons) freshly grated Parmesan cheese
1 small radicchio, finely shredded
drizzling of olive oil and lemon juice, to serve
freshly ground black pepper

- Peel the pears, leaving the stalks intact. Quarter the fruit lengthways and remove the cores. Place the pear quarters in a deep pan with the sugar and cover with the water. Gently bring to the boil, then cover with damp greaseproof paper (the paper should touch the fruit) and reduce the heat. Simmer for 3 minutes until the pears are tender. Drain and cool quickly in iced water.
- Meanwhile, pre-heat the grill to high. Cut the mozzarella into 24 long thick fingers and wrap each in a small piece of Parma ham. Place on a foil-lined grill tray and grill for 3–4 minutes until the cheese is golden. In a small bowl, mix together the butter and Parmesan cheese. Spread over the Parma ham. Grill for 5 minutes.
- Place 2 pear quarters on each serving plate. Add some of the radicchio to each, then top with the grilled mozzarella. Drizzle with a little olive oil and lemon juice and add a grinding of freshly ground black pepper. Serve immediately.

Timballo Abruzzese
Pancake lasagne Abruzzo-style

This traditional Italian recipe is originally from my region of Abruzzo, and is another dish from my wedding menu. Pancakes are used rather than pasta as it's intended to be a starter and therefore lighter than a normal lasagne (although you could use sheets of lasagne instead, if you prefer). The timballo *can also be served cold with salad as a light lunch.*

Serves 8
Preparation time: 45 minutes
Cooking time: 1 hour 20 minutes

300ml (10fl oz) Salsa Besciamella (see page 206)

For the Bolognese sauce
30ml (2 tablespoons) olive oil
1 onion, peeled and finely chopped
1 carrot, peeled and chopped
1 celery stick, chopped
1 garlic clove, peeled and crushed
1 sprig of fresh rosemary
350g (12oz) pork mince
150ml (5fl oz) red wine
1 x 400g (14oz) can plum tomatoes

For the meatballs
100g (4oz) pork mince
1 egg yolk
30ml (2 tablespoons) freshly grated Parmesan cheese
15ml (1 tablespoon) dried breadcrumbs
salt and freshly ground black pepper
plain flour for coating
vegetable oil for shallow frying

For the pancakes
1 egg yolk
300ml (10fl oz) milk
15ml (1 tablespoon) olive oil
100g (4oz) plain flour
600ml (1pint) milk

50g (2oz) butter

To assemble
120ml (8 tablespoons) freshly grated Parmesan cheese
1 egg yolk
300ml (10fl oz) milk

- First make the Bolognese sauce. Heat the oil in a large pan and fry the onion for 2–3 minutes until soft. Stir in the carrot, celery, garlic and rosemary sprig and cook for a further 3–4 minutes. Add the mince and cook for 4–5 minutes, stirring well to break up any clumps. Add the wine and simmer for 3 minutes. Stir in the plum tomatoes, breaking the tomatoes up with a spoon. Leave to simmer for 45 minutes.
- Meanwhile, make the meatballs. Place the mince in a bowl and mix in the egg yolk, Parmesan cheese and breadcrumbs. Season with salt and freshly ground black pepper. Mould the mixture into about 30 small balls and coat them well with flour. Shallow fry the meatballs in hot vegetable oil until golden brown all over. Drain on kitchen paper and set aside until required.
- For the pancakes, place the egg yolk in a jug and add the milk, olive oil, a pinch of salt and some freshly ground black pepper. Place the flour in a bowl and make a well in the centre; gradually beat in the milk mixture to make a smooth batter.
- Heat a little of the butter in a 25cm (10in) non-stick frying pan until hot. Add a small ladleful of batter and tilt the pan to spread the batter evenly. Cook for 1–2 minutes until golden brown on the base and set on top. Flip the pancake over and cook for a further 1–2 minutes. Remove from the pan. Continue to make 10 pancakes in total.
- Pre-heat the oven to 190°C, 375°F, Gas Mark 5. To assemble the lasagne, lightly grease a deep ovenproof lasagne dish. Mix the Bolognese sauce with the béchamel sauce, and spread a little of the mixed sauces on the bottom of the prepared dish. Cover with a layer of pancakes, spread with a little more sauce and then scatter over some of the meatballs and Parmesan cheese. Mix together the egg yolk and milk and drizzle some of this over the meatballs. Continue to layer the ingredients in this way. Finish with pancakes and sauce, sprinkled with the remaining Parmesan cheese.
- Bake for 25–30 minutes until the top is golden brown and crisp. Allow to stand for 5 minutes before serving.

Carrè d'Agnello al Rosmarino
Rack of lamb with rosemary

I do like using this particular cut of lamb for roasting, although if you are cooking for lots of people you might prefer to roast a whole leg. In my family, we would roast the whole lamb, with fresh hard herbs, such as bay leaf, and garlic

Serves 8
Preparation time: 20 minutes
Cooking time: 45 minutes

1.4kg (3lb) medium-sized baking potatoes, peeled and quartered
120ml (8 tablespoons) olive oil
900g (2lb) baby carrots with green fronds, most of green trimmed
8 baby aubergines
4 garlic cloves, lightly crushed
8 small racks of lamb, each with 4 cutlets
100g (4oz) dried breadcrumbs
2 sprigs of fresh rosemary, stalks removed and leaves chopped
30ml (2 tablespoons) chopped fresh flat-leaf parsley
30ml (2 tablespoons) chopped fresh sage
1 fresh red chilli, seeded and finely chopped
salt and freshly ground black pepper
30ml (2 tablespoons) smooth mustard

For the gravy
15ml (1 tablespoon) balsamic vinegar
150ml (5fl oz) red wine
150ml (5fl oz) vegetable stock
25g (1oz) butter

- Pre-heat the oven to 190°C, 375°F, Gas Mark 5. Bring a large pan of water to the boil. Add the potatoes and parboil for 5 minutes, then drain.
- Place 60ml (4 tablespoons) of the oil in a large roasting tin and heat in the oven for 5 minutes until almost smoking. Quickly add the potatoes to the tin and shake about to coat with the hot oil. Add the carrots, aubergines and garlic. Roast for 15 minutes.
- Meanwhile, heat the remaining oil in another roasting tin on top of the hob and sear the racks of lamb all over for 5–8 minutes. Turn the racks bone side down. Transfer the tin to the oven and roast the lamb for 10 minutes.

- In a large bowl, mix together the breadcrumbs, herbs and chilli and season with salt and freshly ground black pepper.
- Spread the mustard over the thin layer of fat on the tops of the racks of lamb and press the breadcrumb mixture on the mustard. Return to the oven and roast for a further 5 minutes until the lamb is cooked to your taste. Allow to rest while making the gravy.
- Pour off and discard as much fat as possible from the roasting tin, then place it on the hob. Add the vinegar to the pan and deglaze, scraping all the bits of meat and sediment off the bottom. Stir in the red wine and stock and boil for 5 minutes until syrupy. Away from the heat whisk in the butter. Strain through a sieve. Season to taste with salt and freshly ground black pepper.
- Serve the lamb with the vegetables and gravy.

Meringhe Morbide
Soft meringues with raspberry coulis

This dessert is very similar to the French îles flottantes, or Floating Islands, except the poached meringues are served on a raspberry coulis rather than a custard. As children, we used to make this as it is very simple and so delicious. It's extremely popular in my restaurants.

Serves 8
Preparation time: 20 minutes
Cooking time: 5 minutes

2 large egg whites
200g (7oz) caster sugar
600ml (1 pint) milk
150ml (5fl oz) water
450g (1lb) raspberries

- Place the egg whites in a large bowl and whisk until firm. Gradually whisk in 125g (5oz) of the caster sugar, 15ml (1 tablespoon) at a time, and continue whisking until the mixture is firm and glossy.
- Place the milk and water in a large wide pan and bring to the boil. Reduce to a simmer. Add heaping tablespoonfuls of the meringue mixture to the milk and poach for 2 minutes on each side until the meringues are set. Gently remove with a slotted spoon and allow to cool, then drain on kitchen paper. Discard the milk.
- Place 400g (14oz) of the rasperries in a food processor with the remaining sugar and process until smooth. Strain the purée through a sieve, discarding the seeds.
- Just before serving, pour the raspberry coulis into a large shallow serving dish and spoon the meringues on top. Decorate with the remaining raspberries to serve.

Ferragosto

Ferragosto falls on 15 August and is supposed to be the hottest day of the year. It is a national holiday in Italy. Normally lunch is the big occasion for family and friends, and this is followed by a long siesta to recharge the batteries in preparation for the many street parties and barbecues in the evening.

Ferragosto is also a religious feast day. In my village, as in many others, statues of the Virgin Mary and other saints are taken through the streets in a procession before returning to the church to be blessed. As my brother is a priest, this day is extremely important to my family, and attendance at church is imperative.

Not only is Ferragosto a great time of year for Italians, it is also exciting for visitors to Italy, who get a chance to experience the traditional festivities and to try many of the festive and regional dishes. The following is typical of the kind of menu served in my village on this special day. Since I come from a fishing village, the menu includes lots of fish. People gather in the village piazza where a group of cooks fries large amounts of fish in a huge pan. This is eaten by all the villagers, washed down with lots of local wine.

Zuppa di Fiori di Zucchini
Chilled courgette flower soup

Courgette blossoms, or flowers, are particularly good at this time of year. They can be prepared in many different ways, but I like them in this soup. Another of my favourites is to stuff the flowers with ricotta cheese and spinach and bake for 20 minutes. This soup is also delicious with the addition of some borlotti beans and served hot. If you only have a few courgette flowers, omit them from the soup and use more courgettes, then garnish each serving with a flower.

Serves 8
Preparation time: 15 minutes plus chilling
Cooking time: 30–35 minutes

300g (11oz) courgette flowers
25g (1oz) butter
1 onion, peeled and chopped
400g (14oz) potatoes, peeled and thinly sliced
1.2 litres (2 pints) vegetable stock
60ml (4 tablespoons) olive oil
2 garlic cloves, peeled and crushed
600g (1¼lb) courgettes, trimmed and thinly sliced
salt and freshly ground black pepper
8–12 fresh basil leaves
16 deep-fried fresh basil leaves, to garnish (optional)

- Gently rinse the courgette flowers to remove any grit. Pat dry on kitchen paper, then cut in half lengthways. Set aside until required.
- Melt the butter in a large pan, add the onion and sauté for 3–4 minutes until just golden. Stir in the potatoes and cook for a further 3 minutes. Add about 150ml (5fl oz) of the stock. Bring to the boil, then simmer for 8–10 minutes until the potatoes soften.
- Meanwhile, heat half of the oil in another pan and add the garlic and the courgettes and their flowers. Cook for 2 minutes, stirring frequently. Add the remaining stock and simmer for 10 minutes.
- Transfer the potato mixture to a food processor and process until smooth and creamy. Pour into the pan with the courgette mixture and whisk together gently. Season well with salt and freshly ground black pepper to taste. Cook for a further 2–3 minutes.
- Leave the soup to cool at room temperature, then place in the refrigerator to chill. Just before serving, roughly chop the basil and stir through the soup. Drizzle with the remaining olive oil and garnish with deep-fried basil leaves, if using.

Spaghetti Scoglio
Spaghetti with shellfish sauce

This was a particularly popular dish when I was a child, as living by the sea we always had a good supply of shellfish. You don't have to use all the fish listed here – just use clams and mussels, if you prefer. But make sure you flavour with good extra virgin olive oil. I introduced my old friend, Paul Simper, to this recipe 12 years ago in my first restaurant, and he's still returning to enjoy this beautiful dish.

Serves 8
Preparation time: 20 minutes
Cooking time: 15 minutes

175g (6oz) mussels
175g (6oz) small clams
350g (12oz) spaghetti
10ml (2 teaspoons) extra virgin olive oil
25g (1oz) butter
1 small red onion, peeled and finely chopped
2 garlic cloves, peeled and crushed
1 small fresh red chilli, seeded and finely chopped
2 bay leaves
2–4 cooked large langoustines in shell
4 cooked Mediterranean prawns in shell
4 cooked crab claws in shell, thawed if frozen
15ml (1 tablespoon) brandy
50ml (2fl oz) dry white wine
50ml (2fl oz) fish stock
30ml (2 tablespoons) chopped fresh flat-leaf parsley
15ml (1 tablespoon) chopped fresh dill
4 fresh sage leaves, finely chopped
salt and freshly ground black pepper

- Scrub the mussels and clams, scraping off any barnacles and pulling off the beards. Discard any mussels and clams that remain open when tapped on a hard surface. Set aside until required.
- Bring a large pan of salted water to the boil. Add the spaghetti and cook for 7 minutes, or according to the instructions on the packet, until *al dente*.
- Meanwhile, heat the oil and butter in a large frying pan. Add the red onion and sauté for 2–3 minutes until just soft. Stir in the garlic, chilli, bay leaves and all the shellfish. Cook for 1

minute. Quickly add the brandy and ignite to flambé. Once the flames have died down, add the wine and stock. Cover the pan and cook for 3 minutes until the mussels and clams have opened. Stir in the chopped herbs and season to taste with salt and freshly ground black pepper.

- Drain the pasta, then either mix it into the shellfish sauce, or divide the spaghetti among the serving plates or bowls, piling it in a tall mound in the centre, and spoon over the shellfish sauce. Serve immediately, with more freshly ground black pepper.

Christmas. Top left: *Antipasti Misti* (page 188); top right: *Maiale Castagnolo* (page 191); bottom left: *Vin Santo;* bottom right: *Panettone ai Mirtilli* (page 194)

Carnevale di Venezia. Top left: *Sformatini di Zucchini* (page 196); top right: *Fegato alla Veneziana e Fichi* (page 198); bottom left: *Focaccia* with onions and tomatoes (page 216); bottom right: *Frittelle alle Mele* (page 199)

Some Italian ingredients. Top left: *Bresaola di Tonno* (Air-dried tuna); top right: *Tartufo Bianco* (White Truffles); bottom left: Wood-smoked Mozzarella; bottom right: Red basil

Top left: *Fichi al Forno* (page 175); top right: *Mascarpone alla Pera* (page 174);
bottom right: *Tortine di Cioccolato* (page 176)

Orata al Cartoccio
Whole roast sea bream in paper

This roasted sea bream is one of the first recipes I cooked on TV, and therefore must be dedicated to Bruce Burgess, pictured on the back cover of this book, who was brave enough to put me in front of the camera for the first time. For a complete course, serve the fish with steamed or roast new potatoes and a salad of bitter leaves dressed with lemon juice and olive oil.

Serves 8
Preparation time: 30 minutes
Cooking time: 20 minutes

8 x 225g (8oz) small sea bream, cleaned
freshly ground black pepper
4 garlic cloves, peeled and sliced
8 sprigs of fresh rosemary, broken into smaller sprigs
120ml (8 tablespoons) dried breadcrumbs
10ml (2 teaspoons) flaked sea salt
100g (4oz) stoned black olives, halved
150ml (5fl oz) fish stock
150ml (5fl oz) dry white wine
100g (4oz) butter
2 lemons, sliced

- Pre-heat the oven to 200°C, 400°F, Gas Mark 6. Season the fish all over with freshly ground black pepper, rubbing the cavities with the seasoning too. Using a sharp knife, make 2 slits on one side of each fish and fill these with garlic and rosemary.
- Place each fish on a large piece of greaseproof paper and sprinkle with breadcrumbs, salt flakes and olives. Wrap the fish in the greaseproof paper. Place the parcels on baking sheets and roast for 10 minutes.
- Open the greasproof paper. Drizzle the fish with the stock and wine and dot with the butter. Return to the oven, unwrapped, and roast for a further 10 minutes. To check if the fish is cooked, insert the point of knife in the flesh; if the blade comes out warm the fish is ready.
- Serve immediately, garnished with lemon slices.

Coniglio Affogato alla Molisana
Skewers of rabbit and pork sausage

Rabbit was a staple food in my family. We always ate it roasted with rosemary, garlic and white wine, but I much prefer it this way! Rabbit is now readily available in butchers and supermarkets.

Serves 8
Preparation time: 20 minutes plus marinating
Cooking time: 15 minutes

350ml (12fl oz) white wine vinegar
350ml (12fl oz) water
44 fresh sage leaves
2 sprigs of fresh rosemary
salt and freshly ground black pepper
900g (2lb) rabbit meat, cut into bite-sized pieces
30ml (2 tablespoons) chopped fresh rosemary
45ml (3 tablespoons) chopped fresh flat-leaf parsley
16 thin slices of Parma ham
4 fresh Italian sausages, each cut into 4
125ml (4fl oz) virgin olive oil

- Place the vinegar and water in a bowl with the sage leaves and rosemary sprigs. Season well with salt and freshly ground black pepper. Add the rabbit meat and mix well. Cover and marinate for 12–24 hours in the refrigerator. Stir occasionally.
- Drain the rabbit, reserving the sage leaves. Season the rabbit with a little salt and plenty of freshly ground black pepper. Sprinkle with the chopped rosemary and half of the parsley; mix well.
- Cut the Parma ham into small pieces, each one large enough to wrap a piece of rabbit. Wrap the rabbit with the ham. Thread 3 pieces of wrapped rabbit on to each of 16 skewers, alternating the rabbit with pieces of sausage and sage leaves from the marinade.
- Make a charcoal fire in a barbecue, pre-heat the grill to high or heat a griddle. Brush the skewers with oil and barbecue, grill or cook on the griddle for 15 minutes until tender and cooked through. Turn and brush with oil frequently during the cooking. Serve immediately, sprinkled with the remaining parsley.

Gelato alla Pesca
Fresh peach ice cream

Make sure you buy fragrant ripe peaches to ensure a good flavour. If you like, serve the ice cream with a simple sauce made from brown sugar and lemon and orange juices.

Serves 8
Preparation time: 10 minutes plus freezing

350g (12oz) fresh ripe peaches, peeled, quartered and stoned
300ml (10fl oz) condensed milk
grated zest and juice of 1 lemon
300ml (10fl oz) whipping cream

To serve
fresh peach slices
wafer-style biscuits

- Place the peaches in a food processor with the condensed milk, lemon zest and juice and whipping cream. Process until smooth.
- Pour the ice cream mixture into a 1.2 litre (2 pint) freezerproof container. Freeze for 2 hours until mushy.
- Turn out into a chilled bowl and mash with a fork to break up the ice crystals. Pour the ice cream back into the freezerproof container and freeze for 3–4 hours until firm.
- Remove the ice cream from the freezer about 30 minutes before required and allow to soften slightly. Serve scoops of the ice cream with fresh peach slices and wafer-style biscuits.

Ferragosto

Autumn/Winter

Pizza Pane alla Caprese
Pan-fried pizza bread

Very simple, this can be served as a starter or can be used as bread. My friend Natalie Imbruglia, who is enjoying great success at the moment with her new record, isn't a big eater, but loves this when I make it for her.

Serves 4
Preparation time: 10 minutes
Cooking time: 13 minutes

450g (1lb) self-raising flour
15ml (1 tablespoon) salt
freshly ground black pepper
5ml (1 teaspoon) dried oregano or 30ml (2 tablespoons) chopped fresh marjoram
150ml (5fl oz) olive oil, plus extra for greasing
120ml (8 tablespoons) water

For the topping
4 plum tomatoes, skinned and thinly sliced
1 x 125g (5oz) buffalo mozzarella cheese, drained and cut into cubes
90ml (6 tablespoons) chopped fresh basil
flaked sea salt for sprinkling
60ml (4 tablespoons) olive oil

- Sift the flour and salt into a large bowl and stir in some pepper and the oregano or marjoram. Add the olive oil and water and mix to form a firm dough. Turn out on to a floured surface and knead for 5 minutes until the dough is smooth and springs back when gently pressed with your finger.
- Roll out the dough until large enough to fit into an ovenproof frying pan about 25cm (10in) diameter. Heat the frying pan and grease it well with olive oil. Add the pizza dough and cook for 5 minutes until golden brown on the base and risen slightly. Flip the pizza base over and cook for a further 5 minutes until golden on the other side.
- Pre-heat the grill to medium-hot. Arrange the tomato slices on the pizza base (still in the pan) and scatter the mozzarella over the top. Grill for 3 minutes until the cheese is melted and bubbling.
- Sprinkle with the basil and salt flakes, then drizzle with the oil. Cut into wedges to serve.

Tortine con fave e pomodoro
Broad bean and tomato tarts

These are an excellent first course for a large party, or can be nibbles with pre-dinner drinks.

Makes 12
Preparation time: 15 minutes
Cooking time: 10 minutes

50g (2oz) butter, cubed
5–6 *grissini* (bread sticks), lightly crushed
125g (5oz) podded fresh broad beans
1 beef tomato, seeded and cubed
3 eggs
125ml (4fl oz) milk
60ml (4 tablespoons) chopped fresh flat-leaf parsley
salt and freshly ground black pepper

- Pre-heat the oven to 200°C, 400°F, Gas Mark 6. Using some of the butter, grease a 12-hole patty tray. Sprinkle the crushed *grissini* into the patty holes.
- Blanch the broad beans in a pan of boiling salted water for 3 minutes. Drain and skin the beans, if necessary. Mix the beans with the tomato.
- Beat the eggs in a bowl with the milk, parsley and a seasoning of salt and freshly ground black pepper.
- Divide the bean mixture among the patty holes, then spoon in the egg mixture. The patty holes should only be half filled.
- Bake the tarts for 10 minutes until just set. Allow to stand for 5 minutes before removing from the tin. Serve warm or cold.

Frittata al Pomodoro e Peperoni
Italian-style tomato and pepper omelette

Frittata was a very popular dish in my family, because it can be used to make the most of all the left-over cooked vegetables from the day before.

Serves 4
Preparation time: 10 minutes
Cooking time: 15–20 minutes

60ml (4 tablespoons) olive oil
3 ripe medium tomatoes, chopped
1 onion, peeled and finely chopped
2 peppers (1 green and 1 yellow), seeded and thinly sliced
salt and freshly ground black pepper
5 eggs
60ml (4 tablespoons) chopped fresh basil leaves

- Heat 30ml (2 tablespoons) of the oil in a large frying pan, add the tomatoes and cook for 2 minutes, stirring. Add the onion and peppers and season with salt and freshly ground black pepper. Cook for 10 minutes, stirring frequently. Tip the vegetables into a bowl. If necessary, wipe out the frying pan with kitchen paper.
- Beat the eggs in a bowl. Heat the remaining oil in the frying pan and add the eggs. Scatter over the basil and top with the fried vegetables. Cover tightly with a lid and cook over a low heat for 5 minutes until the frittata is set. Serve warm or cold.

Mozzarella alla Pizzaiola
Fried mozzarella with pizza sauce

Mozzarella is a great cheese to use for cooking, but save buffalo mozzarella to serve simply dressed with olive oil and basil.

Serves 4
Preparation time: 15 minutes
Cooking time: 20 minutes

45ml (3 tablespoons) olive oil
1 garlic clove, peeled and crushed
4 plum tomatoes, skinned and chopped
4 anchovy fillets, chopped
15ml (1 tablespoon) capers
60ml (4 tablespoons) plain flour
salt and freshly ground black pepper
2 eggs
500g (1lb 2oz) dried breadcrumbs
2 x 125g (5oz) mozzarella cheeses, drained and halved
vegetable oil for deep-frying
6 fresh basil leaves, chopped
60ml (4 tablespoons) chopped fresh flat-leaf parsley
15ml (1 tablespoon) chopped fresh oregano or marjoram
fresh basil leaves, to garnish

- Heat the oil in a pan, add the garlic and tomatoes and cook for 2 minutes, stirring. Stir in the anchovies and capers and simmer for 10 minutes.
- Meanwhile, place the flour on a plate and season with salt and freshly ground black pepper. On another plate, beat the eggs. Spread the breadcrumbs on a third plate. Pat the mozzarella pieces dry, then coat all over with the flour, followed by the eggs and, finally, the breadcrumbs.
- Heat enough vegetable oil in a deep pan for deep-frying. The oil is hot enough when it reaches 160–180°C, 325–350°F on a frying thermometer or when a piece of bread dropped into the oil will sizzle and brown in 30 seconds. Gently lower the mozzarella into the hot oil, cooking in 2 batches, and fry for 4 minutes on each side. Drain on kitchen paper.
- Stir the chopped herbs into the anchovy sauce and season to taste with salt and freshly ground black pepper. Spoon the sauce on to warmed serving plates and top each with a piece of deep-fried mozzarella. Garnish with the fresh basil leaves to serve.

Pizzette Saporite
Mini pizzas party-style

Pizza has to be the most popular Italian food – perfect for all occasions. A regular in Zilli Bar is my friend Kieran O'Brien, who could often be found enjoying one of our pizzas when off the set of Cracker.

Makes 12 mini pizzas
Preparation: 25 minutes
Cooking time: 10–15 minutes

2 x 125g (5oz) packets pizza base mix
1 x 400g (14oz) can plum tomatoes
5ml (1 teaspoon) dried oregano
2.5ml (½ teaspoon) garlic salt
salt and freshly ground black pepper
1 x 125g (5oz) mozzarella cheese, drained and cubed
4 thin slices of Parma ham
8–12 mussels, steamed open and shelled
8 asparagus tips
2 sun-dried tomatoes in olive oil, sliced
2 sun-dried peppers in olive oil, sliced
30ml (2 tablespoons) olive oil

- Pre-heat the oven to 220°C, 425°F, Gas Mark 7.
- Make up the pizza base mixture according to packet instructions. Knead the dough on a lightly floured surface for 5 minutes until smooth. Roll out on a lightly floured surface as thinly as possible and cut out 12 x 7.5cm (3in) rounds. Place on greased baking sheets.
- Sieve the tomatoes into a large bowl and add the oregano, garlic salt and salt and freshly ground black pepper to taste. Spread 5–10ml (1–2 teaspoons) of the tomato sauce on each pizza base and top with mozzarella cubes. Top 4 of the pizza bases with ruffled Parma ham, another 4 with mussels and the remainder with asparagus tips, tomatoes and peppers.
- Drizzle all the pizzas with a little olive oil and bake for 10–15 minutes until the mozzarella is golden brown and the base is crisp. Serve warm.

Panzerotti
Deep-fried stuffed pizzas

*A great way of using up left-over pizza dough. You can be very adventurous with your fillings –
try marinated vegetables, spinach or diced spicy sausages as alternatives to the mixture
suggested here.*

Makes 8 pizzas
Preparation time: 30 minutes
Cooking time: 40 minutes

1 x 400g (14oz) can chopped tomatoes
salt and freshly ground black pepper
2 x 125g (5oz) packets pizza base mix
1 x 125g (5oz) mozzarella cheese, drained and cubed
25g (1oz) Parmesan cheese, freshly grated
50g (2oz) pancetta, cubed
vegetable oil for deep-frying

- Place the tomatoes in a pan and cook for 30 minutes until a thick pulp is formed. Season
  well with salt and freshly ground black pepper. Leave until cold.
- Meanwhile, make up the pizza base mixture according to packet instructions. Knead the
  dough on a lightly floured surface for 5 minutes until smooth. Roll out on a lightly floured
  surface and cut out 8 x 10cm (4in) rounds.
- Spread the tomato over the pizza dough, leaving a border clear round the edge. Top with
  the mozzarella, Parmesan and pancetta. Brush the edges of each round with water, then
  fold over to make a half moon shape and press the edges together to seal.
- Heat enough oil in a deep pan for deep-frying. The oil is hot enough when a piece of the
  dough dropped into the oil sizzles and becomes golden brown in 45 seconds. Add the
  parcels, in batches of 2 or 3, and fry for 2–3 minutes on each side until golden brown.
  Drain on kitchen paper and serve hot.

Ceci e Patate
Chickpea and potato soup

A good soup served as a starter before a roast dinner or excellent as a light lunch with a salad. When I'm on a health drive, I always opt for soups, particularly vegetable-based ones which are both nutritious and tasty.

Serves 4
Preparation time: 25 minutes
Cooking time: 40 minutes

450g (1lb) yellow waxy potatoes
60ml (4 tablespoons) olive oil
1 medium Spanish onion, peeled and finely chopped
1 fennel bulb, trimmed and finely chopped
2 celery sticks, trimmed and finely chopped
2 carrots, peeled and finely chopped
4 garlic cloves, peeled and crushed
1 small fresh red chilli, seeded and finely diced
175g (6oz) chorizo, skinned and finely diced
2 sprigs of fresh thyme
1 bay leaf
2 litres (3¼ pints) hot chicken stock
2 x 400g (14oz) cans chickpeas, drained
pinch of saffron threads, soaked in a little boiling water to infuse
15ml (1 tablespoon) tomato purée
salt and freshly ground black pepper
45ml (3 tablespoons) chopped fresh flat-leaf parsley

- Place the potatoes in a large pan of water and bring to the boil. Cook for 15 minutes until just tender. Drain and leave to cool slightly.
- Meanwhile, heat the oil in a deep pan and add the onion, fennel, celery, carrots, garlic and chilli. Cook for 5–8 minutes until the vegetables just begin to brown, stirring occasionally.
- Stir the chorizo, thyme sprigs and bay leaf into the vegetable mixture. Reduce the heat, cover with a damp piece of greaseproof paper (so the oil in the chorizo will sweat out) and put on the lid. Cook for 5 minutes.
- Peel the boiled potatoes and dice the flesh. Add the potatoes to the vegetables together with the stock, chickpeas, saffron and tomato purée. Stir to mix. Bring to the boil, then reduce the heat and simmer, covered with the lid, for 15 minutes.
- Season the soup and stir in the parsley. Serve immediately.

Zuppa d'Orzo
Barley soup

This is a delicious soup, well worth spending the time to make, and it will keep for a good 24 hours if refrigerated. It is wonderful served piping hot on a winter's evening. Don't be put off by the chilli – it won't blow your head off, but just adds a delightful spike of hotness. Serve the soup with some of the wonderful Italian breads now available.

Serves 4–6
Preparation time: 25 minutes plus soaking
Cooking time: 35–40 minutes

400g (14oz) pearl barley
60ml (4 tablespoons) extra virgin olive oil, plus more to serve
1 medium onion, peeled and finely chopped
2 medium leeks, trimmed and finely chopped
2 garlic cloves, peeled and crushed
1 medium fresh red chilli, seeded and chopped, or 2 small dried chillies, crumbled
½ head of celery, trimmed and finely chopped
1 fennel bulb, trimmed and finely chopped
4 beef tomatoes, skinned, seeded and chopped
2 litres (3¼ pints) vegetable stock
1 bay leaf
2 sprigs of fresh thyme
salt and freshly ground black pepper
juice of 1 lemon
450g (1lb) baby spinach, washed and roughly chopped
30ml (2 tablespoons) chopped fresh flat-leaf parsley
45ml (3 tablespoons) chopped fresh mint

- Place the barley in a bowl and cover with boiling water. Leave to soak for 1 hour. Drain the barley and rinse with cold water. Set aside.
- Place the oil in a deep pan and add the onion, leeks, garlic, chilli, celery and fennel. Stir well, then cover with a damp piece of greaseproof paper (the paper should touch the vegetables) and put on the lid. Place over a very low heat and sweat the vegetables for 10 minutes. The vegetables will soften but should not brown.
- Stir the tomatoes into the vegetables and cook, uncovered, for 5 minutes. Add the stock, bay leaf, thyme and barley, and season with salt and freshly ground black pepper. Bring to the boil, then reduce the heat and simmer for 20–25 minutes until the barley is tender.
- Discard the bay leaf and thyme. Ladle one-third of the soup into a food processor and

process to a purée. Return the purée to the remaining soup and add the lemon juice and spinach. Stir well; the heat from the soup will wilt the spinach. Add the parsley and mint.

• Serve immediately, drizzled with more extra virgin olive oil.

Minestrone al Prosciutto
Traditional minestrone with ham

Parma ham is essential to a good minestrone (although if you are a vegetarian, please feel free to leave out the ham). This hearty vegetable-based soup, a favourite of mine, can be a meal in itself, served with freshly grated Parmesan.

Serves 6
Preparation time: 25 minutes
Cooking time: 30 minutes

15ml (1 tablespoon) olive oil
1 thick slice of Parma ham, weighing about 100g (4oz), cut into sticks
1 medium onion, peeled and finely chopped
2 garlic cloves, peeled and finely chopped
2 celery sticks, trimmed and finely chopped
2 carrots, peeled and finely diced
1 large courgette, trimmed and finely diced
½ small Savoy cabbage, shredded
1.5 litres (2¾ pints) chicken stock
1 bay leaf
15ml (1 tablespoon) tomato purée
1 x 400g (14oz) can cannellini beans, drained and rinsed
salt and freshly ground black pepper
100g (4oz) baby spinach leaves
30ml (2 tablespoons) chopped fresh flat-leaf parsley
freshly grated Parmesan cheese, to serve

- Heat the oil in a large deep pan, add the Parma ham and cook for 2 minutes. Stir in the onion, garlic, celery and carrots. Cook for 5 mintues until the vegetables are soft and just beginning to brown.
- Stir the courgette and cabbage into the vegetable mixture and cook for a further 2 minutes. Add the stock, bay leaf and tomato purée and stir well. Bring to the boil, then reduce the heat and simmer for 10 minutes.
- Stir the cannellini beans into the soup and season with salt and plenty of freshly ground black pepper. Simmer for a further 10 minutes until all the vegetables are very tender.
- Away from the heat, stir the spinach and parsley into the soup; the heat of the soup will cook the spinach. Serve with plenty of grated Parmesan cheese and more freshly ground black pepper sprinkled over the top.

Ribollita
Tuscan white bean soup

This makes a good main course. It is a thick, winter soup and one that my family used to eat with mozzarella, salami and lots of crusty bread. The Italian name means 'reboiled' because the soup would once have been made with left-over vegetables.

Serves 6
Preparation time: 25 minutes
Cooking time: 35–40 minutes

60ml (4 tablespoons) extra virgin olive oil
1 medium Spanish onion, peeled and finely chopped
1 medium leek, trimmed and finely chopped
2 carrots, peeled and finely chopped
1 celery stick, trimmed and finely chopped
2 garlic cloves, peeled and crushed
1 sprig of fresh thyme
1 sprig of fresh rosemary
1 bay leaf
4 beef tomatoes, skinned, seeded and roughly chopped
15ml (1 tablespoon) tomato purée
2 litres (3¼ pints) vegetable stock
2 x 400g (14oz) cans cannellini beans, drained and rinsed
2 large potatoes, peeled and diced
salt and freshly ground black pepper
20ml (4 teaspoons chopped fresh parsley
450g (1lb) spinach, washed and roughly chopped
100g (4oz) Parmesan cheese, freshly grated

- Place the oil in a large deep pan and add the onion, leek, carrots, celery, garlic and herbs. Cover with a damp piece of greaseproof paper (the paper should touch the vegetables) and put on the lid. Cook (sweat) the vegetables over a gentle heat for 10 minutes until soft but not browned. Stir in the tomatoes and tomato purée. Cook for 5 minutes.
- Stir in the stock, cannellini beans and potatoes and season well with salt and freshly ground black pepper. Bring to the boil, then reduce the heat and simmer for 20 minutes until the potatoes are very tender.
- Away from the heat, stir in the parsley, spinach and grated Parmesan cheese, and adjust the seasoning if necessary. Serve immediately, with more freshly ground black pepper sprinkled over the top.

Zuppa Arrosto
Roast pumpkin soup with fried pumpkin seeds

A great soup in the autumn, when pumpkins and other squashes are in abundance. The colour is beautiful.

Serves 4–6
Preparation time: 20 minutes
Cooking time: 2 hours

1 medium pumpkin, about 1kg (2¼lb), or 2 medium butternut squashes
30ml (2 tablespoons) olive oil
1 onion, peeled and chopped
2 celery sticks, trimmed and chopped
1 carrot, peeled and chopped
3 garlic cloves, peeled and chopped
1 bay leaf
1.2 litres (2 pints) vegetable stock
salt and freshly ground black pepper
15g (½oz) butter
75g (3oz) skinned pumpkin seeds
2.5ml (½ teaspoon) flaked sea salt

- Pre-heat the oven to 180°C, 350°F, Gas Mark 4. Place the whole pumpkin or butternut squashes in the oven and roast for 1½ hours until soft to the touch.
- Halve the pumpkin or butternut squashes, scoop out the seeds and fibres and discard. Scoop the flesh from the skin and place in a large bowl; set aside.
- Place the oil in a deep pan and stir in the onion, celery, carrot, garlic and bay leaf. Cover with damp greaseproof paper (the paper should touch the vegetables) and put on the lid. Cook (sweat) over a gentle heat for 7–10 minutes until the vegetables are tender but not browned.
- Stir the roasted pumpkin or squash flesh into the vegetables together with the stock and season well with salt and freshly ground black pepper. Bring to the boil, then reduce the heat and simmer, uncovered, for 10–15 minutes until all the vegetables are very tender.
- Meanwhile, melt the butter in a frying pan, add the pumpkin seeds and fry for 3–5 minutes until toasted. Stir in the sea salt.
- Discard the bay leaf and transfer the soup to a food processor. Process until smooth. Return the soup to the pan and heat through, adjusting the seasoning if necessary.
- Serve sprinkled with the toasted pumpkin seeds.

Zuppetta di Cozze
Fresh mussel soup

Mussels are surprisingly cheap and make a delicious soup. I also like them steamed open, then sprinkled with crisp fried breadcrumbs, garlic, herbs and Parmesan cheese, and grilled for 5 minutes. When buying mussels, it is important that their shells are tightly closed (indicating that they are fresh and alive); clean them by scraping off the 'beards' with a small sharp knife.

Serves 4
Preparation time: 25 minutes
Cooking time: 20–25 minutes

1kg (2¼lb) mussels, cleaned
50ml (2fl oz) dry white wine
50g (2oz) unsalted butter
2 shallots, peeled and finely chopped
1 small fresh red chilli, seeded and finely diced
10ml (2 teaspoons) plain flour
900ml (1½ pints) fish stock
125ml (4fl oz) double cream
24 fresh basil leaves, roughly torn
salt and freshly ground black pepper
crusty bread, to serve

- Place the mussels in a large pan and add the wine. Cover tightly and cook over a high heat for 3–4 minutes, shaking the pan occasionally, until the mussels have opened. Discard any mussels that remain closed.
- Drain the mussels in a colander set in a bowl, shaking the colander well to drain any juices trapped in the shells. Shell two-thirds of the mussels. Cover all the mussels and set aside until required. Reserve the cooking liquid.
- Heat half of the butter in a large pan. Stir in the shallots and chilli and fry for 2 minutes until soft but not browned. Meanwhile, mix the remaining butter with the flour to make a paste. Set aside.
- Add the fish stock and mussel cooking liquid to the shallots and bring to the boil. Simmer for 10 minutes. Reduce the heat and add the cream. Gradually stir in the butter paste to thicken the soup. Add the basil and simmer for 5 minutes.
- Return all the mussels to the pan and season well with salt and freshly ground black pepper. Cook for 2–3 minutes to heat through. Serve with crusty bread.

I Tre Fagioli
Three bean soup

Ideally, dried borlotti and cannellini beans should be used for this soup, but as they need to be soaked overnight and then boiled for 1–2 hours I suggest canned beans in this quick version. The combination of the three beans gives variation in colour, flavour and texture. My friends Jeanette and Tony Calliva have a large family, and this is one of their favourite meals.

Serves 4–6
Preparation time: 20 minutes
Cooking time: 35 minutes

90ml (6 tablespoons) olive oil
50g (2oz) pancetta, diced
1 medium onion, peeled and finely chopped
1 celery stick, trimmed and finely chopped
1 carrot, peeled and finely diced
2 garlic cloves, peeled and crushed
1 bay leaf
1 sprig of fresh rosemary, tough stalk discarded and leaves finely chopped
1 x 400g (14oz) can chopped plum tomatoes
1 litre (1¾ pints) vegetable stock
1 x 400g (14oz) can borlotti beans, drained and rinsed
1 x 400g (14oz) can cannellini beans, drained and rinsed
100g (4oz) French beans, trimmed and cut into 2cm (¾in) pieces
100g (4oz) small pasta shapes, such as penne or rigatoni broken in half
salt and freshly ground black pepper
30ml (2 tablespoons) chopped fresh flat-leaf parsley
freshly grated Parmesan cheese, to serve

- Heat 60ml (4 tablespoons) of the oil in a deep pan, add the pancetta and fry for 3 minutes. Stir in the onion, celery, carrot, garlic, bay leaf and rosemary. Cook for 3 minutes, stirring occasionally.
- Stir in the tomatoes and stock. Bring to the boil, then simmer for 15 minutes. Add the canned beans and cook for a further 5 minutes. Discard the bay leaf.
- Ladle half of the soup into a food processor and blend until smooth. Return to the remaining soup in the pan and stir in the French beans and pasta. Season with salt and freshly ground black pepper. Cook for 5–8 minutes until the pasta is *al dente*.
- Away from the heat, stir in the parsley and remaining oil. Adjust the seasoning if necessary and serve with Parmesan cheese.

Zuppa di Asparagi
Asparagus soup with roasted asparagus tips

Asparagus is now available all year, imported from all round the world, but I think English asparagus in season is the best, being delicate and full of flavour. Roasted asparagus tips finish off this soup perfectly.

Serves 4
Preparation time: 20 minutes
Cooking time: 30 minutes

450g (1lb) asparagus
75g (3oz) butter
1 red onion, peeled and finely chopped
1 garlic clove, peeled and crushed
1 large potato, peeled and diced
1 bay leaf
1 large courgette, trimmed and chopped
1.2 litres (2 pints) vegetable or chicken stock
30ml (2 tablespoons) freshly grated Parmesan cheese
salt and freshly ground black pepper
150ml (5fl oz) double cream
30ml (2 tablespoons) chopped fresh flat-leaf parsley

- Trim the asparagus, discarding the woody ends. Cut off the tips, about 5cm (2in), and reserve. Chop the remaining asparagus.
- Melt 50g (2oz) of the butter in a large deep pan and stir in the onion, garlic, potato and bay leaf. Sauté for 3 minutes. Add the chopped asparagus and courgette and cook for 2 minutes, stirring occasionally.
- Add the stock. Bring to the boil, then simmer for 15 minutes until the potatoes are very tender.
- Meanwhile, preheat the oven to 190°C, 375°F, Gas Mark 5. Place the asparagus tips in a roasting tin. Dot with the remaining butter and sprinkle with the Parmesan cheese and plenty of freshly ground black pepper. Roast for 5–8 minutes until the asparagus tips are tender and the cheese has melted.
- Transfer the soup to a food processor and blend until smooth. Return to the pan and add the cream and parsley. Stir well. Season to taste with salt and freshly ground black pepper. Cook for 2–3 minutes until heated through. Serve hot, garnished with the roasted asparagus tips.

Crema di Zucca e Lenticchie Rosse
Cream of marrow, red lentil and sage soup

A great vegetarian dish, this makes the most of lentils and of marrow, which is a vegetable often avoided. In fact, because marrow grows well in the British climate, it is cheap to buy and can be used to make a good low-cost meal. I'm very fond of lentils too, especially served as a side dish simply flavoured with fried onions and garlic.

Serves 4
Preparation time: 25 minutes
Cooking time: 50 minutes

450g (1lb) vegetable marrow, peeled, seeded and diced
60ml (4 tablespoons) extra virgin olive oil
50g (2oz) butter
1 onion, peeled and finely chopped
1 celery stick, trimmed and finely chopped
1 carrot, peeled and finely diced
100g (4oz) white cabbage, shredded
2 garlic cloves, peeled and chopped
4 fresh sage leaves, finely chopped
1 sprig of fresh rosemary, stalk discarded and leaves chopped
100g (4oz) red lentils
2.5 litres (4 pints) vegetable stock
salt and freshly ground black pepper
40g (1½oz) instant polenta flour
75ml (5 tablespoons) milk or cream
freshly grated Parmesan cheese, to serve

- Bring a large pan of water to the boil. Add the marrow and return to the boil, then reduce the heat and simmer for 15 minutes until the marrow is just tender.
- Meanwhile, place 30ml (2 tablespoons) of the oil and 25g (1oz) of the butter in a deep pan and heat until frothy. Stir in the onion, celery, carrot, cabbage, garlic, sage and rosemary. Sauté the vegetables for 5 minutes. Drain the marrow and add to the pan with the lentils. Cook over a high heat for 3 minutes, stirring frequently.
- Stir in three-quarters of the stock and season well with salt and freshly ground black pepper. Bring to the boil, then reduce the heat and simmer for 20 minutes until the lentils are tender.
- Gently heat the remaining oil and butter in a small pan and stir in the polenta flour. Cook for 1 minute, stirring constantly. Away from the heat, gradually stir in the milk or cream and

then the remaining stock. Return to the heat and cook for 2–3 minutes until slightly thickened.

- Stir the thickened mixture into the lentil soup and adjust the seasoning to taste. Cook for a final 2 minutes, then serve with freshly grated Parmesan cheese.

Crema di Merluzzo Affumicato Con Uova
Cream of smoked haddock and poached egg

Although this is not a particularly Italian soup, I like it because it is quite light, and I love serving it with garlic croutons for a crunchy contrast. Be sure to use oak-smoked haddock, which has a true flavour and colour. This soup works perfectly well without the eggs. It's good as a starter or main course.

Serves 4
Preparation time: 20 minutes
Cooking time: 25 minutes

50g (2oz) butter
1 medium Spanish onion, peeled and finely sliced
1 bay leaf
1 large potato, peeled and finely diced
600ml (1 pint) milk
450g (1lb) oak-smoked haddock fillets, skinned and roughly chopped
300ml (10fl oz) whipping cream
salt and freshly ground black pepper
5ml (1 teaspoon) vinegar
4 large eggs
60ml (4 tablespoons) snipped fresh chives

- Melt the butter in a deep pan and add the onion and bay leaf. Cover and cook for 5–8 minutes until the onion softens and begin to caramelise. Stir in the potato and milk. Bring to just below boiling point, then reduce the heat and simmer for 10–12 minutes until the potato is just tender.
- Add the fish to the pan and cook for a further 3 minutes. Discard the bay leaf.
- Pour the soup into a food processor and blend until smooth. Return to the pan and stir in half of the cream. Season to taste. Gently heat through for 5 minutes.
- Meanwhile, add the vinegar to a large pan of boiling water and reduce the heat so the water is simmering. Gently break the eggs into the water, one at a time, and poach for 2–3 minutes. Remove with a slotted spoon and drain on kitchen paper.
- Combine the remaining cream with 6 turns of the peppermill and whip until very soft peaks form. Ladle the soup into 4 warmed serving bowls and gently swirl in the whipped cream. Top each bowl with a poached egg and sprinkle with the chives to serve.

Garlic croutons: Cut diagonal slices from a French stick. Rub them with a cut garlic clove and drizzle with a little olive oil, then toast on each side. Allow 1 or 2 croutons per person.

Zuppa di Spinaci e Patate
Spinach and potato soup

A nutritious dish for all the family, this is hearty and perfect for a winter lunch with crusty bread. It's a favourite with children, as demonstrated by my daughter Laura and her friends, who love it.

Serves 4
Preparation time: 15 minutes
Cooking time: 20–25 minutes

450g (1lb) potatoes, peeled and diced
1.2 litres (2 pints) vegetable or chicken stock
25g (1oz) butter
1 medium onion, peeled and finely chopped
2 garlic cloves, peeled and thinly sliced
100ml (4fl oz) single cream
450g (1lb) spinach, washed and roughly chopped
pinch of freshly grated nutmeg
salt and freshly ground black pepper

- Place the potatoes in a deep pan with the stock and bring to the boil. Cook for 15 minutes until very tender. Do not drain.
- Meanwhile, melt the butter in another deep pan and add the onion and garlic. Cover with damp greaseproof paper (the paper should touch the onion) and put on the lid. Cook (sweat) over a very low heat for 5 minutes until the onion is soft but not browned.
- Stir the cream into the onion mixture, then transfer to the pan containing the potatoes. Stir in the spinach and season well with the nutmeg and salt and freshly ground black pepper to taste. Cook for 3 minutes until the spinach is just wilted. (Do not allow to boil or the cream may separate.) Serve immediately with more freshly ground black pepper.

Finocchio Rosolato
Sautéed Fennel

Fennel is one of my favourite vegetables. I love it sautéed this way, which is one of the easiest and most delicous ways of cooking it, but I also love it raw with virgin olive oil and salt as a salad. Being so versatile, fennel is good steamed or roasted and used in sauces and dressings.

Serves 4
Preparation time: 5 minutes
Cooking time: 10 minutes

4 fennel bulbs
15ml (1 tablespoon) olive oil
50g (2oz) butter
10ml (2 teaspoons) fennel seeds
60ml (4 tablespoons) water
salt and freshly ground black pepper

- Slice the root end from each fennel bulb and discard. Quarter each bulb lengthways.
- Heat the oil and butter in a large frying pan. Add the fennel, fennel seeds and water. Bring to the boil and cook over a high heat for 8–10 minutes until the fennel is tender and the cooking juices are reduced to a syrup. Season to taste with salt and freshly ground black pepper. Serve hot.

Spinaci all'Aglio, Olio e Peperoncino
Fresh spinach with garlic, chilli and Parmesan

This is a good winter dish, healthy and with a little chilli heat. I like it sprinkled with lots of freshly grated Parmesan cheese. Frozen spinach can also be used; just thaw and drain it well.

Serves 4
Preparation time: 5 minutes
Cooking time: 10 minutes

1.8kg (4lb) spinach, washed and tough stalks discarded
30ml (2 tablespoons) olive oil
75g (3oz) butter
2 garlic cloves, peeled and crushed
1 fresh red chilli, seeded and finely chopped
salt and freshly ground black pepper
100g (4oz) Parmesan cheese, freshly grated

- Place the spinach leaves in a large heavy-based saucepan (do not add any extra water – the water clinging to the leaves from washing is sufficient). Cover the pan and cook gently for 6–7 minutes until the spinach wilts; stir occasionally to prevent the leaves from sticking to the pan. The spinach should have shrunk to one-quarter of its original volume. Drain well and allow to cool slightly, then squeeze out excess water. Roughly chop the spinach.
- Heat the oil in a large heavy-based pan. Add the butter and cook until bubbling and frothy. Stir in the garlic and chilli and fry for 2 minutes. Add the spinach and season to taste with salt and freshly ground black pepper. Cook until heated through.
- Sprinkle over the Parmesan cheese and serve immediately.

Broccoli al Burro con Capperi
Sautéed broccoli with butter and capers

Broccoli can be quite bland if served plain, but butter and capers give it a lift. This dish is an ideal partner for fish, particularly sea bass and red mullet. Another vegetable that is good with capers is cauliflower, with chopped anchovies and olive oil instead of butter.

Serves 4
Preparation time: 5 minutes
Cooking time: 10 minutes

450g (1lb) broccoli florets
75g (3oz) butter
75g (3oz) capers
salt and freshly ground black pepper

- Bring a large pan of salted water to the boil. Add the broccoli and blanch for 4 minutes. Drain.
- Heat 50g (2oz) of the butter in a large frying pan, add the broccoli and sauté for 5 minutes until tender. Remove with a slotted spoon to a serving dish and keep warm.
- Add the remaining butter to the pan juices and heat to melt. Stir in the capers and cook for 1 minute until heated through. Season with salt and freshly ground black pepper. Spoon over the broccoli and serve.

Patate Cipolline
Baked potato with chives, red onion and pine nuts

For extra richness, spoon mascarpone cheese over each baked potato just before serving.
Alternatively, for added Italian flavour, fill the potatoes with ricotta cheese and spinach or
Parma ham.

Serves 4
Preparation time: 5 minutes
Cooking time: 1 hour

4 baking potatoes, scrubbed and pricked
60ml (4 tablespoons) pine nuts
1 red onion, peeled and finely chopped
45ml (3 tablespoons) chopped fresh chives
salt and freshly ground black pepper

- Pre-heat the oven to 180°C, 350°F, Gas Mark 4. Place the potatoes on a baking tray and bake for 1 hour until soft to the touch.
- Meanwhile, heat a heavy-based frying pan, add the pine nuts and dry-fry for 3–4 minutes, shaking and stirring constantly, until golden brown. Transfer the pine nuts to a small bowl and mix in the onion and chives.
- Slit the baked potatoes open and season with salt and freshly ground black pepper, then spoon in the pine nut mixture. Serve immediately.

Polenta ai Funghi
Stewed flat mushrooms in wine with polenta

I remember this dish from my childhood. I used to help my mother prepare it and then enjoyed the results with all the family. It's a great side dish for steak or game, and easy to make.

Serves 4
Preparation time: 15 minutes
Cooking time: 35 minutes

For the polenta
1.75–2 litres (3–3½ pints) water
5ml (1 teaspoon) salt
350g (12oz) polenta flour
125g (5oz) butter
200g (7oz) Parmesan cheese, freshly grated

For the mushroom topping
45ml (3 tablespoons) olive oil
1 small onion, peeled and finely chopped
1 garlic clove, peeled and crushed
8 very large flat mushrooms, wiped clean and sliced
60ml (4 tablespoons) chopped fresh flat-leaf parsley
salt and freshly ground black pepper
125ml (4fl oz) dry white wine
8 fresh basil leaves, chopped

- To prepare the polenta, place the water in a large deep pan, add the salt and bring to the boil. Reduce the heat and gradually add the polenta flour to the water, stirring constantly with a whisk. When the polenta is completely blended in, simmer for 20 minutes, stirring occasionally, until the polenta is very dense and thick and is coming away from the sides of the pan.
- Meanwhile, make the topping. Heat the oil in a large frying pan, add the onion and garlic and gently fry for 5 minutes until soft and just beginning to brown. Stir in the mushrooms and parsley and fry for a further 5–8 minutes until the mushrooms are golden brown. Season well with salt and freshly ground black pepper. Add the wine and simmer for 5 minutes. Remove from the heat and stir in the basil. Adjust seasoning to taste.
- Beat the butter and Parmesan cheese into the polenta and sprinkle with plenty of freshly ground black pepper. Divide the polenta among 4 warmed serving plates and spoon over the mushrooms. Serve immediately.

Salsicce in Casseruola con Polenta
Italian sausage casserole with polenta

A great winter dish when you are cooking on a tight budget. Buy the sausages from a good local Italian deli.

Serves 4
Preparation time: 25 minutes
Cooking time: 45 minutes

45ml (3 tablespoons) olive oil
1 onion, peeled and chopped
2 garlic cloves, peeled and chopped
450g (1lb) carrots, peeled and finely diced
1 celery heart, trimmed and diced
2 leeks, trimmed and finely chopped
1 red pepper, seeded and diced
8 fresh Italian sausages, such as luganeghe or salsicce
300ml (10fl oz) white wine
1 cooking apple, cored, peeled and finely chopped
1 bay leaf
salt and freshly ground black pepper
45ml (3 tablespoons) chopped fresh flat-leaf parsley

For the polenta
1.75–2 litres (3–3½ pints) water
5ml (1 teaspoon) salt
350g (12oz) polenta flour
125g (5oz) butter
200g (7oz) Parmesan cheese, freshly grated

- Heat the oil in a large deep pan. Add the onion, garlic, carrots, celery, leeks and red pepper. Stir well and cook for 5–8 minutes until the vegetables are just turning golden brown. Add the sausages and fry for 3 minutes. Add the wine, apple and bay leaf and season to taste with salt and freshly ground black pepper. Bring to the boil, then reduce the heat and simmer for 15 minutes. If all the juices evaporate, add more wine or some stock.
- Meanwhile, prepare the polenta (see page 217). Away from the heat, beat in the butter and Parmesan cheese. Season to taste with salt and plenty of freshly ground black pepper.
- Divide the polenta among 4 large serving plates and top with the sausage casserole. Sprinkle with the flat-leaf parsley to serve.

Polenta Sfiziosa

Party polenta crostini

A great starter or party nibble. The toppings can easily be changed according to the occasion. I particularly like this recipe as it uses a good selection of Mediterranean vegetables, which give superb colour and flavour.

Serves 4
Preparation time: 25 minutes
Cooking time: 35 minutes

For the polenta
1.75–2 litres (3–3½ pints) water
5ml (1 teaspoon) salt
350g (12oz) polenta flour
200g (7oz) Parmesan cheese, freshly grated
olive oil for brushing

For the toppings
3 plum tomatoes, skinned, seeded and diced
1 garlic clove, peeled and finely chopped
6 fresh basil leaves, roughly torn
60ml (4 tablespoons) extra virgin olive oil
flaked sea salt and freshly ground black pepper
350g (12oz) mixed vegetables, such as courgettes, peppers and aubergine, trimmed
5ml (1 teaspoon) fresh thyme leaves
15ml (1 tablespoon) balsamic vinegar
75g (3oz) dolcelatte cheese, sliced
6 thin slices of Parma ham, each halved

- First prepare the polenta (see page 217).
- Beat the Parmesan cheese into the polenta. Spread the polenta in a large baking tray to make a layer about 2.5cm (1in) thick. Leave to cool.
- Meanwhile, make the toppings. For the tomatoes *al crudo*, place the tomatoes in a bowl and stir in the garlic, basil and 30ml (2 tablespoons) of the oil. Season well with salt and freshly ground black pepper.
- For the marinated grilled vegetables, thinly slice the mixed vegetables into long strips. Heat a griddle until smoking, then add the remaining oil and place the vegetables on the griddle. Cook for 3–4 minutes on each side until golden brown. Transfer to a bowl and season with salt, freshly ground black pepper and the thyme leaves. Add the balsamic vinegar.

- Once the polenta is cool and solid, cut it into thick, long fingers. Pre-heat the grill to hot. Brush the polenta fingers with olive oil and place on a foil-lined grill pan. Toast the polenta under the grill for 2 minutes on each side until golden brown and crisp.
- Top one-third of the polenta fingers with the dolcelatte cheese and ruffled-up Parma ham. Grill for a further 2 minutes until the cheese is melted and bubbling.
- Top another third of the polenta fingers with the tomatoes *al crudo*, and the remainder with the mixed grilled vegetables. Serve the polenta crostini on a large platter or wooden boards.

Polenta

Polenta al Pomodoro e Ricotta
Polenta with fresh tomato, basil and ricotta

This used to be one of my favourite dishes when I first moved away from home and had to cook for myself on a low budget. It's still a favourite today. The tomato and ricotta sauce is also good served with pasta.

Serves 4
Preparation time: 20 minutes plus setting
Cooking time: 45 minutes

For the polenta
1.75–2 litres (3–3½ pints) water
5ml (1 teaspoon) salt
350g (12oz) polenta flour
200g (7oz) Parmesan cheese, freshly grated
olive oil for brushing

For the sauce
30ml (2 tablespoons) olive oil
2 shallots, peeled and finely chopped
2 garlic cloves, peeled and crushed
8 plum tomatoes, skinned, seeded and roughly chopped
5ml (1 teaspoon) light soft brown sugar
salt and freshly ground black pepper
100g (4oz) ricotta cheese, mashed
8 fresh basil leaves, chopped
sprigs of fresh basil, to garnish

- First prepare the polenta (see page 217). Beat the Parmesan cheese into the polenta. Spread the polenta in a large baking tray to make a layer about 2.5cm (1in) thick. Leave to cool.
- Meanwhile, make the sauce. Heat the oil in pan, add the shallots and gently fry for 3–5 minutes until soft. Stir in the garlic and cook for a further 1 minute. Add the tomatoes and sugar and stir well. Cook for 15 minutes until the tomatoes become a pulp. Season well with salt and freshly ground black pepper. Beat in the ricotta cheese and chopped basil.
- Once the polenta is cool and solid, cut it into squares. Pre-heat the grill to hot. Brush the polenta squares with oil and place on a foil-lined grill pan. Grill the polenta for 2 minutes on each side until golden brown and crisp.
- Spoon the tomato and ricotta sauce on to warmed serving plates and place the grilled polenta on top. Garnish with basil sprigs and sprinkle with more pepper to serve.

Coniglio e Polenta
Rabbit with wild mushrooms and grilled polenta

Polenta and rabbit are the perfect combination, and this rabbit stew accompanied by grilled polenta is a good alternative to the traditional family Sunday roast. Rabbit is often overlooked in England, although it is popular in other European countries. Try it for yourself to see how good it is.

Serves 4
Preparation time: 30 minutes plus marinating overnight
Cooking time: 35 minutes

1 large rabbit, skinned and cleaned
1 x 75cl bottle red wine
1 bay leaf
1 sprig of fresh thyme
45ml (3 tablespoons) olive oil
6 shallots, peeled and finely chopped
2 garlic cloves, peeled and finely chopped
450g (1lb) baby carrots, scrubbed clean
5ml (1 teaspoon) chilli oil
salt and freshly ground black pepper
450g (1lb) fresh wild mushooms, wiped clean and sliced if necessary
25g (1oz) butter
30ml (2 tablespoons) chopped fresh flat-leaf parsley

For the polenta
1.75–2 litres (3–3½ pints) water
5ml (1 teaspoon) salt
350g (12oz) polenta flour
200g (7oz) Parmesan cheese, freshly grated
olive oil for brushing

- Cut the rabbit into quarters, or even smaller pieces if liked. Place in a large plastic container and add the wine, bay leaf and thyme. Cover tightly and leave to marinate in the refrigerator overnight.
- Heat the oil in large, deep, heavy-based pan, add the shallots and cook over a gentle heat for 5–8 minutes until soft. Stir in the garlic and cook for a further 1 minute. Add the rabbit with its marinade, the carrots and the chilli oil. Season with salt and freshly ground black pepper. Bring to the boil, then reduce the heat and simmer for 25 minutes. If the liquid

reduces too much, add some meat stock or water. Add half of the mushrooms to the rabbit half-way through cooking. At the end of the cooking time, the rabbit should be very tender.

- While the rabbit is cooking, prepare the polenta (see page 217). Beat the Parmesan cheese into the polenta. Spread the polenta in a large baking tray to make a layer about 2.5cm (1in) thick. Leave to cool.
- Once the polenta is cool and solid, cut it into squares. Pre-heat the grill to hot. Brush the polenta squares with oil and place on a foil-lined grill pan. Grill the polenta for 2 minutes on each side until golden brown and crisp.
- At the same time, heat the butter in large frying pan, add the remaining wild mushrooms and sauté for 4–5 minutes. Stir in the parsley and fry for a further 1 minute.
- To serve, spoon the rabbit stew into 4 large serving bowls. Top with the sautéed mushrooms and serve with the grilled polenta.

Struzzo al Pepe Rosa
Ostrich steaks in pink peppercorn sauce

My restaurant in Dean Street was one of the first to put ostrich on the menu when beef was receiving bad publicity, and it has been a great success. Ostrich meat is quite brown in colour so it looks rather like beef, but it has a more 'gamey' flavour. Ostrich is something people rarely cook at home, but I recommend that you be a little adventurous and try this recipe.

Serves 2
Preparation time: 25 minutes
Cooking time: 25–30 minutes

60ml (4 tablespoons) pink peppercorns, roughly crushed
2 x 225g (8oz) ostrich steaks
60ml (4 tablespoons) olive oil
450g (1lb) sweet potatoes, peeled
2 heads of chicory, halved lengthways
1 red pepper, seeded and cut into thin strips
salt and freshly ground black pepper
50g (2oz) butter
15ml (1 tablespoon) brandy
200ml (7fl oz) single cream
15ml (1 tablespoon) Worcestershire sauce
125ml (4fl oz) red wine

- Preheat the oven to 200°C, 400°F, Gas Mark 6, and pre-heat the grill to high.
- Press the crushed peppercorns all over the steaks. Heat 30ml (2 tablespoons) of the oil in a large frying pan, add the steaks and cook for 5 minutes on each side until golden brown.
- Meanwhile, prepare the vegetables. Place the sweet potatoes in a pan of water and bring to the boil. Reduce the heat and simmer for 10 minutes. At the same time, cook the chicory in a separate pan of boiling water for 8–10 minutes; drain.
- Drain and slice the sweet potatoes. Heat 15 ml (1 tablespoon) of the olive oil in an ovenproof frying pan, add the sweet potatoes and red pepper and sauté for 3 minutes. Transfer the pan to the oven and roast for 5–8 minutes until tender and golden brown.
- Meanwhile, place the chicory on a foil-lined grill pan. Drizzle with the remaining olive oil and season with salt and freshly ground black pepper. Cook the chicory under the hot grill for 5–8 minutes until beginning to brown.
- Remove the steaks from the pan. Wipe the pan clean, then melt the butter in it and return the steaks. Add the brandy and ignite to flambé. Once the flames die down, stir in the cream, Worcestershire sauce and wine. Simmer for 5 minutes until the sauce thickens.

- To assemble, place 2 chicory halves in the centre of each warmed serving plate. Place a steak on each and spoon the sauce over the top. Serve with the roasted sweet potatoes and pepper.

Stufato d'Agnello ai Carciofi
Lamb and artichoke stew

This is definitely a meat dish for a big occasion, but you'll find it is very easy to make. Serve with polenta, mashed potatoes or even rice, or with puréed root vegetables such as parsnips, carrots, turnips or celeriac.

Serves 4
Preparation time: 20 minutes
Cooking time: 1 hour 10 minutes

4 globe artichokes
juice of 1 lemon
25g (1oz) plain flour
salt and freshly ground black pepper
700g (1½lb) lean boneless lamb (leg or shoulder), cubed
60ml (4 tablespoons) olive oil
2 shallots, peeled and finely chopped
450ml (15fl oz) dry white wine
3–4 sprigs of fresh thyme
3–4 sprigs of fresh mint

- Wash the artichokes, trim the stalks and discard any tough outer leaves. Cut each artichoke lengthways into 6 wedges, and remove the hairy choke with a small spoon. Place the artichokes in a large bowl of water with the lemon juice (this prevents them from discolouring).
- Spread the flour on a plate and season with salt and freshly ground black pepper. Coat the lamb cubes all over with the seasoned flour. Heat the oil in a large deep pan, add the shallots and cook over a gentle heat for 5 minutes until just soft. Add the lamb cubes to the pan and cook over a high heat for 5–8 minutes until browned all over.
- Drain the artichokes and add to the meat. Sauté for 5 minutes. Stir in the wine and herbs. Bring to the boil, then reduce the heat to a simmer, cover and cook for 50 minutes until the meat and artichokes are very tender. Adjust seasoning if necessary and serve.

Entrecot in Casseruola
Pot roast marinated sirloin of beef

When I first opened Signor Zilli restaurant in Dean Street, I used to arrange entertainment downstairs for the children so their parents could relax over their Sunday lunch. This recipe was always a success with the adults. It is important to get a good cut of beef, not on the bone, and to pay a lot of attention to the cooking.

Serves 8
Preparation time: 20 minutes plus marinating overnight
Cooking time: 2 hours

1 x 1.8kg (4lb) boned sirloin of beef
90ml (6 tablespoons) olive oil
1 onion, peeled and chopped
150g (5oz) pancetta, diced
900g (2lb) field mushrooms
4 plum tomatoes, skinned
15ml (1 tablespoon) Dijon mustard
salt and freshly ground black pepper

For the marinade
3 red onions, peeled and sliced
3 oak-smoked garlic cloves, peeled and crushed
1 x 75cl bottle Chianti
90ml (6 tablespoons) balsamic vinegar
5ml (1 teaspoon) soft brown sugar
4 bay leaves
1 large bouquet garni, consisting of sprigs of fresh basil, parsley, thyme and oregano or
    marjoram, celery and shreds of orange zest

- Mix together the ingredients for the marinade in a large bowl. Add the beef. Cover with cling film and leave to marinate overnight.
- The next day, remove the beef and pat dry with kitchen paper. Strain the marinade and reserve both the liquid and the vegetables and herbs.
- Heat the oil in a flameproof casserole, add the onion and pancetta and sauté on a high heat until the onion is soft and starting to brown. Put the beef in the pan and brown on all sides. Add all the marinade vegetables and herbs. Pour in some of the marinade liquid and stir to deglaze the bottom of the casserole.
- Turn the beef over, and add the mushrooms and tomatoes. Cover the casserole and turn

the heat down to low. Cook for 1 hour, gradually adding the remaining marinade liquid to keep the meat moist.

- Stir in the mustard. Continue cooking for a further 1 hour until the beef is tender. Season with salt and freshly ground black pepper before serving.

Zampone con Lenticchie
Pig's trotters with lentils

Buy zampone, *which is stuffed pig's trotters, from a good Italian deli (they would take far too long to make yourself). The* zampone *come pre-cooked and vacuum-packed, and just need to be boiled for 20 minutes. Although this dish has been making regular appearances on London restaurant menus over the last few years, it is still quite unusual, and well worth trying at home.*

Serves 2
Preparation time: 20 minutes
Cooking time: 20–25 minutes

1 *zampone*
100g (4oz) red lentils
60ml (4 tablespoons) olive oil
1 medium onion, peeled and finely chopped
2 garlic cloves, peeled and chopped
1 carrot, peeled and finely diced
1 celery stick, trimmed and finely chopped
1 bay leaf
15ml (1 tablespoon) fresh thyme leaves
30ml (2 tablespoons) chopped fresh flat-leaf parsley
10 fresh sage leaves, finely chopped
salt and freshly ground black pepper

- Cook the *zampone* in a pan of boiling water for 20 minutes or according to packet instructions.
- Meanwhile, place the lentils in a separate pan and cover with cold water. Bring to the boil, skimming the surface of any scum, then reduce the heat and simmer for 12–15 minutes until *al dente*. Drain the lentils, reserving 30ml (2 tablespoons) of the cooking liquid.
- Heat 30ml (2 tablespoons) of the olive oil in a large frying pan and add the onion, garlic, carrot, celery, bay leaf and thyme. Cover with damp greaseproof paper (the paper should touch the vegetables) and put on the lid. Cook (sweat) the vegetables for 3–5 minutes until they are soft. Stir in the lentils, parsley, sage, the remaining oil and the reserved lentil cooking liquid. Season well with salt and freshly ground black pepper and heat through.
- Divide the lentils between 2 large serving bowls. Drain the *zampone* and slice into rings. Place on the lentils to serve.

Filetto d'Agnello all'Agrodolce
Grilled lamb fillets with caramelised red onions

Lamb can be prepared in a variety of ways. Good cuts are quick and easy to cook, but don't be put off tougher cuts as they can be marinated first. Caramelised red onions are great with lamb. This dish is always enjoyed when I cook for friends.

Serves 4
Preparation time: 10 minutes
Cooking time: 20–25 minutes

4 medium red onions, peeled and thinly sliced
1 garlic clove, peeled and thinly sliced
1 bay leaf
2 sprigs of fresh thyme
100g (4oz) caster sugar
60ml (4 tablespoons) balsamic vinegar
butter for greasing
4 x 200g (7oz) lamb neck fillets
salt and freshly ground black pepper
15ml (1 tablespoon) olive oil

To serve
fresh thyme leaves
balsamic vinegar

- Place the onions in a large frying pan with the garlic, bay leaf, thyme sprigs, sugar and vinegar. Cover with buttered greaseproof paper (the paper should touch the onions), then put on the lid. Cook over a gentle heat for 20–25 minutes until the onions are soft, glazed and sweet.
- Meanwhile, place the lamb fillets between sheets of cling film and pound with a rolling pin to flatten. Season all over with salt and freshly ground black pepper.
- Just before the onions are ready, pre-heat a griddle on the hob until almost smoking. Add the oil and heat, then place the lamb fillets on the griddle and sear for 2 minutes on each side. Transfer to a warmed plate, cover and leave to stand for 3 minutes.
- Discard the bay leaf and thyme sprigs and spoon the onions into the centre of 4 warmed serving plates. Slice each lamb fillet, place on the piles of onions and garnish with fresh thyme leaves and a drizzle of balsamic vinegar.

Bistecca al Pomodoro
Rump steaks with plum tomato, garlic and herb sauce

Very simple, fast and packed with flavour, this dish is excellent for working couples with a family. I particularly enjoy it in winter. Rump steak is relatively inexpensive, less tender than other steak but very tasty. I would recommend marinating it first in a red wine marinade for 10–15 minutes, if possible. Use organic beef if you are worried about food safety.

Serves 4
Preparation time: 15 minutes
Cooking time: 30 minutes

15ml (1 tablespoon) olive oil
4 x 175g (6oz) rump steaks, trimmed
350g (12oz) button mushrooms, wiped clean and chopped

For the tomato sauce
15ml (1 tablespoon) olive oil
2–3 garlic cloves, peeled and thinly sliced
700g (1½lb) ripe plum tomatoes, skinned and roughly chopped
15ml (1 tablespoon) chopped fresh oregano or 5ml (1 teaspoon) dried oregano
salt and freshly ground black pepper

- First make the tomato sauce. Heat the oil in a small deep pan, add the garlic and fry for 1 minute. Quickly stir in the tomatoes, oregano and salt and freshly ground black pepper to taste. Simmer for 15 minutes until the tomatoes have completely disintegrated.
- Heat the oil in a heavy-based frying pan and add the steaks. Fry for 2 minutes on each side, seasoning well with salt and freshly ground black pepper on turning. Remove the steaks from the pan and set aside.
- Add the mushrooms to the pan and fry over a fierce heat for 3–5 minutes, stirring frequently. Return the steaks to the pan and pour over the tomato sauce. Cook for a further 5 minutes. Serve immediately.

Tagliata alla Diavola
Fillet steak with garlic and chilli sauce

Steak is very popular on Italian menus, usually just simply grilled and served with a well-dressed salad. This recipe is a particular favourite of one of my oldest friends, Nino Ripani, who comes from the same village in Italy as I do. He's a fitness fanatic and loves a good steak.

Serves 4
Preparation time: 25 minutes
Cooking time: 15 minutes

For the Caesar salad
½ ciabatta loaf
125ml (4fl oz) olive oil
6 anchovy fillets
2 garlic cloves, peeled and crushed
10ml (2 teaspoons) Dijon mustard
25g (1oz) Parmesan cheese, freshly grated
5ml (1 teaspoon) Worcestershire sauce
1 egg
1 cos lettuce, separated into leaves and cut or torn into bite-sized pieces
Parmesan cheese shavings, to serve

For the steak
45ml (3 tablespoons) olive oil
1 x 350g (12oz) whole beef fillet
1 small fresh red chilli, seeded and finely chopped
1 sprig of fresh rosemary, tough stalk discarded and leaves finely chopped
1 garlic clove, peeled and finely chopped
1 shallot, peeled and finely chopped
juice of 1 lime
salt and freshly ground black pepper

- Pre-heat the grill to high. Halve the piece of ciabatta lengthways, then cut across each half to make 4 pieces in all. Scrape out the inner soft bread and brush both sides of the crust with some of the olive oil. Toast these croutons under the grill until golden brown on both sides. Set aside to cool.
- Finely chop 2 of the anchovies and set aside. Place the remaining anchovies in a blender and add the garlic, mustard, grated Parmesan, Worcestershire sauce and egg. Blend until smooth. With the blender still running, add the remaining olive oil in a steady stream until

the dressing thickens. Pour into a small bowl and set aside.

- For the fillet steak, pre-heat the oven to 220°C, 425°F, Gas Mark 7. Heat an ovenproof frying pan and add a drizzle of olive oil. Add the beef fillet and sear all over until browned. Transfer the pan to the oven and roast for 8–10 minutes. Leave to rest for 3 minutes.
- Put the remaining olive oil in a small bowl and stir in the chilli, rosemary, garlic, shallot and lime juice. Season well with salt and freshly ground black pepper.
- To assemble, place the lettuce leaves in a large bowl and add the anchovy dressing. Toss to mix. Place a crouton on each serving plate and pile the dressed leaves on top; sprinkle with the chopped anchovies and Parmesan shavings. Thinly slice the fillet steak and divide among the plates, placing it next to the salad. Spoon the chilli mixture over the steak. Serve immediately.

Spiedino d'Agnello ai Funghi
Lamb skewers with mushrooms

This is very easy to prepare. The spiedino *can also be cooked on the barbecue, and then served with lots of chopped fresh coriander and onion. You need eight small wooden skewers, which you should soak first to prevent them from burning.*

Serves 4
Preparation time: 20 minutes plus marinating
Cooking time: 20 minutes

700g (1½lb) shoulder of lamb, trimmed and cut into large chunks
45ml (3 tablespoons) olive oil
grated zest and juice of 2 lemons
1 garlic clove, peeled and crushed
1 bay leaf
2 sprigs of fresh rosemary
1 large red pepper
4 flat mushrooms, wiped clean and quartered
salt and freshly ground black pepper

- Place the lamb chunks in a bowl and mix in 30ml (2 tablespoons) of the oil, the lemon zest and juice, garlic, bay leaf and rosemary. Cover with cling film and leave to marinate for 1 hour at room temperature.
- Meanwhile, pre-heat a large griddle on the hob until smoking. Add a little of the remaining oil and place the pepper on the griddle. Cook for 5 minutes until the pepper is slightly charred in places on all sides. Halve the pepper and discard the core and seeds. Cut the pepper into 8–12 pieces.
- Rub the soaked skewers with salt and freshly ground black pepper. Thread the lamb chunks, pieces of pepper and mushrooms on to the skewers. Brush some of the marinade over the meat and vegetables. Season with salt and freshly ground black pepper.
- Heat the griddle again and add the remaining oil. When it is hot, place the skewers on the griddle. Cook for 12–15 minutes, turning several times and basting frequently with the marinade. The meat should be tender yet still slightly pink in the centre. Serve immediately.

Polpettone Casalinga
Italian beef and pork burgers

You can involve children in making these – get them to roll up their sleeves and help with the mixing. Minced chicken can be used instead of beef and pork, if you prefer.

Serves 4
Preparation time: 10 minutes
Cooking time: 15 minutes

200g (7oz) beef mince
200g (7oz) pork mince
50g (2oz) dried breadcrumbs
50g (2oz) Parmesan cheese, freshly grated
5ml (1 teaspoon) dried oregano
1 egg, beaten
salt and freshly ground black pepper
45ml (3 tablespoons) sunflower oil
1 beef tomato, sliced
1 x 125g (5oz) mozzarella cheese, drained and sliced

- Place the beef and pork mince in a large bowl and mix in the breadcrumbs, Parmesan cheese, oregano, egg and a seasoning of salt and freshly ground black pepper. Divide the mixture into 4 portions and roll each into a ball. Flatten each ball into a thin patty.
- Pre-heat the grill until medium hot. Heat a large frying pan, then add the oil and heat well. Add the burgers and cook for 5 minutes on each side until golden brown.
- Transfer the the burgers to a foil-lined grill pan and top each with tomato and mozzarella slices. Sprinkle with more freshly ground black pepper. Grill until the cheese is melted, bubbling and turning golden brown. Serve immediately.

Agnellino alla Milanese
Lamb cutlets in herbed breadcrumbs

Lamb cutlets are a good choice when you are looking for a quick recipe, whether you grill them, barbecue them or coat them in breadcrumbs to be shallow-fried or baked. The dish here is ideal for an impromptu dinner party, simply served with pasta, and accompanied by a light red wine such as Vino Nobile di Montepulciano. Neil and Caroline Lindsay love these lamb cutlets.

Serves 4
Preparation time: 15 minutes
Cooking time: 15 minutes

1 garlic clove, peeled and finely chopped
5ml (1 teaspoon) dried oregano
24 fresh basil leaves, finely chopped
6 sprigs of fresh rosemary, tough stalks discarded and leaves finely chopped
25g (1oz) fresh mint leaves, finely chopped
100g (4oz) dried breadcrumbs
25g (1oz) plain flour
salt and freshly ground black pepper
4 eggs
12 lamb cutlets or loin chops
vegetable oil for shallow-frying
2 lemons, sliced

- Mix together the garlic, herbs and breadcrumbs in a large bowl. Spread on a large plate. Place the flour on another large plate and season with salt and freshly ground black pepper. Lightly beat the eggs on another large plate.
- First coat the lamb cutlets with the seasoned flour, then with egg and, finally, with the herbed breadcrumbs, pressing the crumbs well on to the meat.
- Heat enough oil for shallow-frying (about 1cm/½ in) in a large frying pan. Add the lamb cutlets and cook for 5–8 minutes on each side. Drain on kitchen paper and allow to stand for 2 minutes before serving, with the lemon slices.

Filetto di Lepre al Ribes
Roast fillet of hare with port and redcurrant sauce

Game, like fish, is a very popular food in my region of Abruzzo. This particular recipe is fairly easy to make; however, I suggest that you buy the hare from a butcher, who will offer good advice if you're not familiar with preparing and cooking hare.

Serves 2
Preparation time: 30 minutes
Cooking time: 20 minutes

275g (10oz) celeriac, peeled
75g (3oz) potatoes, peeled and diced
sunflower oil for deep-frying
25g (1oz) unsalted butter
45–60ml (3–4 tablespoons) milk
salt and freshly ground black pepper
2 x 175g (6oz) fillets of hare, sinew removed
15ml (1 tablespoon) olive oil
90ml (6 tablespoons) port
300ml (10fl oz) hot meat stock
30ml (2 tablespoons) redcurrant jelly

- Pre-heat the oven to 220°C, 425°F, Gas Mark 7. Chop 175g (6oz) of the celeriac and place in a large pan of salted water with the potatoes. Bring to the boil, then cook for 10 minutes until very tender.
- Meanwhile, cut the remaining celeriac into sticks. Heat enough oil in a deep pan for deep-frying until very hot, then deep-fry the celeriac sticks until golden and crisp. Drain on kitchen paper and keep warm.
- Drain the potatoes and celeriac well, then tip into a large bowl and mash with the butter and milk. Season to taste with salt and freshly ground black pepper. Cover and keep warm.
- Season the hare all over with salt and freshly ground black pepper. Heat the olive oil in a large frying pan and add the hare fillets. Cook over a high heat for 5–8 minutes until seared and golden brown all over. Transfer the hare to a baking tray. Leave to stand for 5 minutes.
- Add the port to the pan juices together with the stock and redcurrant jelly. Cook, stirring, until the jelly dissolves, then bring to the boil and boil for 5 minutes until the sauce is reduced slightly and becomes syrupy.
- Roast the hare for 2–5 minutes until cooked to your taste.
- Spoon the mashed vegetables onto 2 hot serving plates. Slice the hare and arrange on the mash, then spoon over the sauce. Garnish with the crisp-fried celeriac to serve.

Piccione ai Porcini
Warm salad of wood pigeon with grilled porcini and puffball

Now that wood pigeons are available throughout the year (from good butchers) this recipe could be prepared in the summer too. Giant puffball is a wild mushroom that is very common in English fields and pastures. It can grow up to a kilo in size. If you cannot find puffball, you can substitute large flat mushrooms.

Serves 2
Preparation time: 20 minutes
Cooking time: 10 minutes

2 young oven-ready wood pigeons
25g (1oz) unsalted butter, softened
salt and freshly ground black pepper
75g (3oz) fresh porcini, sliced
75g (3oz) fresh puffball, sliced
1 large garlic clove, peeled and finely chopped
45ml (3 tablespoons) extra virgin olive oil
juice of 1 lemon
100g (4oz) mixed bitter salad leaves, such as frisée, radicchio and chicory

- Pre-heat the oven to 220°C, 425°F, Gas Mark 7. Smear the pigeons all over with the butter and season with salt and freshly ground black pepper. Place in a roasting tin and roast for 8 minutes.
- Meanwhile, pre-heat the grill to hot. Scatter the mushrooms on a foil-lined grill pan and season with the garlic and a little of the olive oil. Grill for 5–8 minutes until golden. Season with salt and freshly ground black pepper and a little of the lemon juice.
- Divide the salad leaves between 2 large serving plates and top with the mushrooms. Cut the legs and breasts from the pigeons; thinly slice the breast meat. Place the legs and sliced breast meat on the mushrooms and drizzle over the remaining oil and lemon juice to serve.

Capriolo all'Oliva
Roast loin of venison with tapenade and pancetta

This is a good alternative for your Sunday lunch or a special dinner party. It's quite a rich dish, but the combination of flavours works extremely well together. The recipe was given to me by my head chef at Zilli Fish, Ron Irvine. My good chum Trevor Beattie, who is pictured on the back cover, loves all venison dishes and would be delighted with this one.

Serves 6
Preparation time: 30 minutes
Cooking time: 20–25 minutes

60ml (4 tablespoons) virgin olive oil
1 x 1kg (2¼lb) boned loin of venison
150ml (5fl oz) port
150ml (5fl oz) red wine such as Corvo Rosso
30ml (2 tablespoons) redcurrant jelly
100g (4oz) Tapenade (see page 210)
18 thin slices of pancetta
6 juniper berries, crushed
1 large garlic clove, peeled and chopped
salt and freshly ground black pepper
Cavolo Rosso all'Agrodolce (see page 193), to serve

- Pre-heat the oven to 220°C, 425°F, Gas Mark 7. Heat 45ml (3 tablespoons) olive oil in a large heavy-based roasting tin on the hob. Add the loin of venison and fry until seared and golden brown on all sides. Remove the meat and set aside.
- Deglaze the roasting tin with the port and red wine, stirring constantly for 1 minute. Stir in the redcurrant jelly and continue to cook for 2 minutes until the juices are quite syrupy. Transfer this sauce to a small pan and set aside until required.
- Spread the tapenade all over the venison, then wrap in the pancetta. Brush the remaining olive oil on a large piece of baking foil. Sprinkle the juniper berries and garlic over the foil and season with salt and plenty of freshly ground black pepper. Place the venison in the centre and carefully wrap in the foil.
- Set the venison parcel in a clean roasting tin and roast for 15 minutes; the venison should still be rare in the centre.
- Reheat the sauce. Thinly slice the venison and serve with the warm sauce and the cabbage.

Quaglie Ripiene
Roast stuffed quail with a red pepper sauce

This is a dish my customers used to rave about in my very first restaurant. The quails are excellent served with the steamed escarole, porcini and Parmesan salad on page 45. I suggest you buy already boned oven-ready quails as they will then be very quick to stuff.

Serves 2
Preparation time: 20 minutes
Cooking time: 25 minutes

60ml (4 tablespoons) extra virgin olive oil
1 small onion, peeled and finely chopped
1 garlic clove, peeled and finely chopped
50g (2oz) button mushrooms, quartered
25g (1oz) pancetta, diced
4 boned oven-ready quails
salt and freshly ground black pepper
12 thin slices of pancetta
1 large red pepper, seeded and diced
3 plum tomatoes, skinned, seeded and chopped
4 fresh basil leaves

- Pre-heat the oven to 190°C, 375°F, Gas Mark 5. Place 15ml (1 tablespoon) of the olive oil in a frying pan with the onion, half of the garlic, the mushrooms and diced pancetta. Place a piece of damp greaseproof paper over the contents of the pan (the paper should touch the vegetables) and cook (sweat) over a gentle heat for 5 minutes. The onion should be soft but not golden.
- Open out the quails and season with salt and freshly ground black pepper. Spoon the mushroom filling into the quails, then fold them over to enclose the filling. Secure with wooden cocktail sticks. Wrap the pancetta around the quails. Place in a baking tray and roast for 20 minutes.
- Meanwhile, place the red pepper in a food processor with the tomatoes, basil and remaining garlic. Process to a purée. Add the remaining olive oil and process again to mix. Transfer to a pan and season to taste with salt and freshly ground black pepper. Warm through.
- Place the quails on 2 warmed serving plates and spoon the pepper sauce around the birds. Serve immediately.

Faraona alla Romana
Breast of guinea fowl with wild rice and tomato and basil sauce

Guinea fowl, which tastes like slightly gamey chicken, makes a great winter casserole. It is a good alternative to chicken as it has more flavour and a lower fat content.

Serves 4
Preparation time: 20 minutes
Cooking time: 20–30 minutes

225g (8oz) wild rice
4 boned breasts of guinea fowl
45ml (3 tablespoons) extra virgin olive oil

For the sauce
1 onion, peeled and finely diced
45ml (3 tablespoons) extra virgin olive oil
150ml (5fl oz) dry white wine
400g (14oz) plum tomatoes, skinned, seeded and diced
15ml (1 tablespoon) granulated sugar
15ml (1 tablespoon) balsamic vinegar
12 fresh basil leaves, roughly torn
salt and freshly ground black pepper

- Place the wild rice in a large pan and cover with water. Bring to the boil and cook for 20–30 minutes until tender.
- Meanwhile, make the sauce. Place the onion in a frying pan with 15ml (1 tablespoon) of the oil. Cover with damp greaseproof paper (the paper should touch the onion) and cook (sweat) for 5 minutes over a very low heat until the onion is tender but not browned. Stir the wine and tomatoes into the onion and simmer, uncovered, for 1 minute. Stir in the sugar, balsamic vinegar and the remaining oil. Simmer for a further 5 minutes. Away from the heat, stir in the basil leaves and season to taste with salt and freshly ground black pepper. Keep warm.
- Pre-heat the grill to medium-hot. Season the guinea fowl with salt and freshly ground black pepper and place on a foil-lined grill pan. Drizzle with the oil. Grill for 4 minutes on each side until golden brown and tender. Leave to stand for 2–3 minutes.
- Drain the wild rice and season with salt and freshly ground black pepper to taste. Divide the rice among 4 large hot serving plates. Thinly slice each breast of guinea fowl and arrange on the rice. Spoon over the sauce. Serve immediately.

Fagiano Cipollino
Pot-roasted pheasant with baby onions and juniper berries

Pheasants are available from September to February, and when fresh are usually sold as a brace, which is a cock and a hen bird. Juniper berries, which are traditionally used in gin, are the perfect flavouring for the pheasant. This is great served with a risotto or pasta such as pappardelle.

Serves 2
Preparation time: 15 minutes
Cooking time: 50–55 minutes

75g (3oz) unsalted butter, chilled and finely diced
50g (2oz) pancetta, diced
50g (2oz) button mushrooms
150g (5oz) baby onions, peeled
2 sprigs of fresh thyme
1 bay leaf
6 juniper berries, crushed
1 oven-ready pheasant
salt and freshly ground black pepper
250ml (9fl oz) red wine

- Pre-heat the oven to 190°C, 375°F, Gas Mark 5. Using some of the butter, grease a braising or casserole dish, just large enough for the pheasant. Add the pancetta to the dish together with the mushrooms, baby onions, thyme, bay leaf and juniper berries.
- Season the pheasant all over, inside and out, with salt and freshly ground black pepper. Place the pheasant on the vegetables and cover the dish tightly with a lid of baking foil. Roast for 45 minutes until the pheasant is tender.
- Remove the pheasant from the braising dish and set aside in a warm place. Place the braising dish on the hob, add the wine and bring to the boil. Boil for 5 minutes to reduce the juices, then gradually beat in the remaining butter. Adjust the seasoning if necessary.
- Portion the pheasant and place on a large warmed serving plate. Pour over the vegetable sauce and serve immediately.

Faraona al Finocchio
Roast guinea fowl with olives, rosemary and fennel

I think game is under-rated in this country, perhaps because people aren't sure how to cook it at home. This dish shows how easy it can be: simply put all the ingredients in a parcel of foil and roast very slowly. I'm sure you'll be delighted with the result, and that your dinner guests will be impressed. A glass or two of red wine is a must with guinea fowl - try Montepulciano d'Abruzzo.

Serves 2
Preparation time: 20 minutes plus marinating
Cooking time: 45 minutes

1 oven-ready guinea fowl
3 baby fennel bulbs, or 1 large fennel bulb, trimmed and cut into strips
12 stoned black olives
2 sprigs of fresh rosemary
1 large garlic clove, peeled and finely chopped
1 onion, peeled and cut into thin strips
1 celery stick, trimmed and cut into thin strips
1 fresh red chilli, seeded and finely chopped
1 leek, green part discarded, white part cut into strips
juice of ½ lemon
90ml (6 tablespoons) extra virgin olive oil
150ml (5fl oz) dry white wine
salt and freshly ground black pepper

To serve
30ml (2 tablespoons) chopped fresh flat-leaf parsley
extra virgin olive oil
crusty bread

- Joint the guinea fowl: first remove the legs and split each in two (drumstick and thigh). Remove the wishbone from the breasts. You should have 6 pieces.
- Place the guinea fowl in a large bowl and add the fennel, olives, rosemary, garlic, onion, celery, chilli, leek, lemon juice, oil and wine. Mix well and cover with cling film. Leave to marinate for 2 hours at room temperature.
- Pre-heat the oven to 190°C, 375°F, Gas Mark 5. Place the guinea fowl and all the marinade in a large piece of double-thickness baking foil and season with salt and freshly ground black pepper. Bring the foil together to make a parcel. Roast for 45 minutes until the

vegetables and guinea fowl are tender.

- Transfer the the guinea fowl, vegetables and juices to a large dish and sprinkle with the parsley. Drizzle with extra virgin olive oil and serve with plenty of crusty bread.

Capriolo al Ginepro
Venison escalopes with juniper berries and red wine sauce

Venison is a very lean meat, so it doesn't need to be cooked very long. Farmed venison is good and widely available, although wild venison has a more intense flavour. This is excellent served with baked sweet potatoes (see page 55) and spicy spinach (see page 131).

Serves 4
Preparation time: 10 minutes
Cooking time: 20–25 minutes

30ml (2 tablespoons) olive oil
4 x 175g (6oz) venison escalopes cut from the haunch
salt and freshly ground black pepper
300ml (10fl oz) full-bodied red wine
6 juniper berries, crushed
300ml (10fl oz) hot meat stock
30ml (2 tablespoons) redcurrant jelly
15ml (1 tablespoon) arrowroot
50g (2oz) unsalted butter, chilled and finely diced

- Heat the oil in a large frying pan, add the venison escalopes and sear over a high heat for 3–4 minutes on each side until golden brown. Season the venison with salt and freshly ground black pepper on both sides. Remove and set aside.
- Add the wine and juniper berries to the pan juices and bring to the boil, stirring well to mix in the sediment from the bottom of the pan. Boil for 5 minutes until reduced to a syrupy consistency. Add the stock and redcurrant jelly and stir until the jelly melts. Mix the arrowroot with a little water in a small cup until smooth. Stir the arrowroot into the wine mixture and cook until the sauce is thick and clear. Away from the heat, gradually whisk the butter into the sauce.
- Return the venison to the pan and cook gently for 3 minutes until the venison is heated through. Serve immediately.

Gallo Cedrone alle Erbe
Roast grouse with fresh herbs, breadcrumbs and grilled bok choy

This dish is very popular in northern Italy. It's a splendid way to make the most of grouse's short season in the early autumn. A strong red wine for this recipe has to be Barolo; the 1992 vintage would be perfect.

Serves 2
Preparation time: 20 minutes
*Cooking time:*15–20 minutes

2 oven-ready grouse
salt and freshly ground black pepper
30ml (2 tablespoons) olive oil
30ml (2 tablespoons) fresh white breadcrumbs
30ml (2 tablespoons) roughly chopped fresh parsley
30ml (2 tablespoons) snipped fresh chives
1 head bok choy
15–30ml (1–2 tablespoons) wholegrain mustard
juice of ½ lemon

- Pre-heat the oven to 220°F, 425°F, Gas Mark 7. Season the grouse all over, inside and out, with salt and freshly ground black pepper. Heat half of the oil in an ovenproof frying pan, add the grouse and sear over a high heat for 5 minutes until golden brown all over. Transfer the pan to the oven and roast the grouse for 8–10 minutes until the meat is tender yet still pink in the centre. Allow to rest for 5 minutes.
- Meanwhile, mix the breadcrumbs and herbs in a bowl and set aside. Blanch the bok choy in a pan of boiling water for 2 minutes until wilted. Drain the bok choy and refresh in cold water; then pat dry with kitchen paper. Split the bok choy in half lengthways.
- Pre-heat the grill to medium-hot. Cut the legs and breasts from the grouse. Spread the mustard over the skin side of the pieces of grouse, then press the breadcrumb mixture over the mustard. Arrange the pieces of grouse on a foil-lined grill pan. Place the bok-choy halves on the grill pan, cut side up, and drizzle with the remaining oil and the lemon juice. Grill until the crumb coating on the grouse is golden brown.
- Transfer the bok choy to the centre of 2 large hot serving plates and top with the pieces of grouse. Serve immediately

Game

Anatra Selvatica
Wild duck in two styles with orange and lemon sauce

For a romantic candle-lit dinner, this is the ideal choice. It's one of the most popular dishes on the Valentine's Night menus in my restaurants. The Grand Marnier gives the sauce a wonderful flavour and the sweet sauce complements the duck perfectly. Experiment with this dish until you have it just right for you, as duck can be served either rare or well done. Cooking is all about adapting recipes to accommodate your own preferences, so feel free to vary the ingredients too, for example by using different fruits.

Serves 2
Preparation time: 25 minutes
Cooking time: 1 hour

1 oven-ready wild duck
salt and freshly ground black pepper
30ml (2 tablespoons) olive oil
1 bay leaf
1 sprig of fresh rosemary
1 orange
1 lemon
30ml (2 tablespoons) soft brown sugar
30ml (2 tablespoons) red wine vinegar
300ml (10fl oz) hot duck stock or chicken stock
75ml (3fl oz) Grand Marnier
30ml (2 tablespoons) redcurrant jelly
5ml (1 teaspoon) arrowroot
100g (4oz) salad leaves of your choice
extra virgin olive oil, to drizzle

- Remove the legs from the duck and rub them all over with salt and freshly ground black pepper. Place the duck legs in a saucepan, cover with water and add the oil, bay leaf and rosemary. Bring to the boil, skimming the surface of any scum, then reduce the heat and simmer for 1 hour.
- While the legs are cooking, prepare the breasts. Pre-heat the oven to 190°C, 375°F, Gas Mark 5. Place the duck breast, still attached to the carcass, on a baking tray. Season with salt and freshly ground black pepper. Roast for 15 minutes until the breast meat is tender yet still pink in the centre.

- Meanwhile, take one-quarter of the zest from the orange and lemon, shaving it off thinly with a vegetable peeler or knife, then cut the zest into thin strips. Blanch in boiling water for 6 minutes (this removes the bitterness.) Drain and refresh in cold water. Squeeze the juice from both of the fruits and reserve.
- Place the sugar and vinegar in a large frying pan and heat gently to dissolve the sugar. Stir in the stock, Grand Marnier and the orange and lemon zest and juice. Bring to the boil and boil for 5–8 minutes until reduced by half. Add the redcurrant jelly and stir until melted.
- Put the arrowroot in a cup with a little water and mix to a smooth paste. Remove the sauce from the heat and stir in the arrowroot mixture. Return to the heat and cook until thick and glossy, stirring constantly. Season to taste with salt and freshly ground black pepper. Keep the sauce warm.
- Remove the duck breasts from the carcass and place in the sauce, turning to coat all over. Transfer the duck breasts to 2 large serving plates. Pile the salad leaves next to the breasts, drizzle with a little extra virgin olive oil and top with the drained poached duck legs. Serve immediately, with the remaining sauce.

Coniglio in Bellavista
Crown of rabbit with pancetta, grilled polenta and a red pepper sauce

Ask your butcher to prepare the rabbit for you – the two joints should resemble small racks of lamb. This dish serves 2, but rabbit is also a good choice when entertaining several friends. Simply roast the rabbit whole with herbs and olive oil. I would recommend serving this with sautéed fennel (see page 130) and baked potato with chives, red onion and pine nuts (see page 133).

Serves 2
Preparation time: 25 minutes
Cooking time: 8–10 minutes

1 oven-ready rabbit, split lengthways, leaving only the fillets with the cleaned rib bones attached (the legs can be frozen for use in another dish)
6 thin slices of pancetta
60ml (4 tablespoons) extra virgin olive oil
salt and freshly ground black pepper
1 small red pepper, seeded and roughly chopped
1 small garlic clove, peeled and chopped
6 fresh basil leaves
2 x 7.5cm (3in) round slices of set polenta (see page 217), at least 2.5cm (1in) thick
deep-fried basil leaves, to garnish (optional)

- Pre-heat the oven to 200°C, 400°F, Gas Mark 6. Curve each rabbit fillet joint round, with the rib bones pointing outwards, and bring the ends together to make a crown roast. Tie the ends together with butcher's string to secure them tightly. Wrap the pancetta around the meat of each crown, securing it with wooden cocktail sticks if necessary. Cover the ends of the rib bones with foil to prevent them from burning.
- Place the 2 crowns of rabbit on a baking tray. Drizzle with 5ml (1 teaspoon) of the oil and season with salt and freshly ground black pepper. Roast for 8–10 minutes until the meat is tender yet still pink in the centre. Leave to rest for 5 minutes.
- Meanwhile, place the red pepper, garlic and basil leaves in a food processor and process until smooth. Reserve 5ml (1 teaspoon) of the remaining olive oil and add the rest to the pepper paste. Process to make a sauce. Season with salt and freshly ground black pepper.
- Preheat the grill to medium-hot. Place the polenta on a foil-lined grill pan and brush with the remaining oil. Grill the polenta for 2 minutes on each side until golden brown and crisp.
- Place each piece of polenta on a warmed serving plate and top each with a crown of rabbit. Spoon the sauce around the polenta. Garnish with deep-fried basil, if using, and serve.

Coniglio della Nonna
Braised rabbit with black olives and sun-dried tomatoes

This is my Grandmother's recipe, which she made with her own dried tomatoes. I have adapted the recipe to give it a modern touch, and recommend that you try it as it is delicious. Farmed rabbits are generally larger than wild ones; the flesh is paler and therefore has less flavour.

Serves 4
Preparation time: 30 minutes
Cooking time: 2 hours 20 minutes

2 oven-ready rabbits, rib cage and forelegs removed
50g (2oz) plain flour
salt and freshly ground black pepper
30ml (2 tablespoons) olive oil
100g (4oz) pancetta, diced
1 onion, peeled and chopped
100g (4oz) celery, trimmed and chopped
1 x 75cl bottle full-bodied red wine
600ml (1 pint) stock made from rabbit trimmings, or meat stock
30ml (2 tablespoons) balsamic vinegar
12 halves sun-dried tomatoes preserved in oil
24 stoned black olives
1 bay leaf
15ml (1 tablespoon) arrowroot
8 fresh basil leaves

- Pre-heat the oven to 180°C, 350°F, Gas Mark 4. Remove the hind legs from the rabbit and cut the saddle across into 4 sections. Spread the flour on a plate and season with salt and freshly ground black pepper. Roll the 6 rabbit pieces in the seasoned flour to coat all over.
- Heat the oil in a large frying pan. Add the rabbit pieces, in batches, and sear over a high heat for 5–7 minutes until golden brown all over. Transfer the rabbit to a casserole dish.
- Add the pancetta to the frying pan together with the onion and celery. Fry for 3–5 minutes until golden brown. Add the red wine and stir well, scraping all the sediment from the bottom of the pan. Add the stock and balsamic vinegar and bring to the boil. Pour the contents of the pan over the rabbit in the casserole and add the tomatoes, olives and bay leaf. Season with salt and freshly ground black pepper.
- Cover the casserole tightly with a lid or foil. Cook in the oven for 2 hours until the rabbit is

very tender.

- Put the arrowroot in a small cup and mix with a little water to a paste. Stir into the casserole juices and return to the oven to cook for a further 10 minutes. Add the basil leaves and serve immediately.

Capriolo all'Oliva (page 156)

Polenta Sfiziosa (page 136)

Risotto d'Orzo e Porcini in Gabbia (page 35)

Tagliata alla Diavola (page 149)

Salsicce di Salmone
Fresh salmon, spinach and ricotta sausages

These sausages are perfect served with creamy scrambled eggs, to make a delicious breakfast. A healthy alternative to the traditional fry-up.

Makes 16 sausages
Preparation time: 10 minutes
Cooking time: about 10 minutes

225g (8oz) fresh spinach, washed and tough stalks removed
900g (2lb) salmon fillets, skinned
225g (8oz) ricotta cheese
50g (2oz) Parmesan cheese, freshly grated
2 pinches of freshly grated nutmeg
salt and freshly ground black pepper
4m (4⅓yd) natural sausage skins, soaked, rinsed in cold water and cut into 25cm (10in) lengths
30–45ml (2–3 tablespoons) olive oil

- Bring a large pan of water to the boil. Add the spinach all at once and blanch for 1 minute until the leaves wilt. Drain, then squeeze out as much water as possible. Finely chop the spinach and set aside.
- Using tweezers, remove any remaining tiny bones from the salmon. Roughly chop the salmon. Place in a food processor and process until minced. Add the salmon to the spinach together with the ricotta and Parmesan cheeses, nutmeg and a seasoning of salt and freshly ground black pepper. Mix well.
- Spoon the salmon mixture into a piping bag without a nozzle. Tie a knot at one end of each piece of sausage skin, then pipe in the mixture, leaving a 7.5cm (3in) gap to allow for shrinkage. Tie a knot at the other end of the skin.
- Blanch the sausages in a pan of boiling water for 3 minutes. Drain and pat dry on kitchen paper.
- Heat the olive oil in a large frying pan, add the sausages and cook for 3–5 minutes until golden brown all over. Serve with more salt and freshly ground black pepper.

Maiale alle Mele
Pork and apple sausages

Pork and apple are a popular combination, and make delicious sausages flavoured with mace and sage. Use for mixed grills or barbecues, or cut up and add to the Tuscan white bean soup, Ribollita (see page 121).

Makes 16 sausages
Preparation time: 20 minutes plus chilling
Cooking time: about 15 minutes

90ml (6 tablespoons) olive oil
2 onions, peeled and finely chopped
2 Granny Smith apples, cored, peeled and finely chopped
1kg (2¼lb) trimmed belly pork
100g (4oz) fresh white breadcrumbs
pinch of ground mace
1 egg, beaten
5 fresh sage leaves, finely chopped
salt and freshly ground black pepper
4m (4⅓yd) natural sausage skins, soaked, rinsed in cold water and cut into 25cm (10in) lengths

- Heat 45ml (3 tablespoons) of the oil in a large frying pan, add the onions and apples and sauté for 5–8 minutes until very soft. Allow to cool.
- Roughly chop the belly pork, then place in a food processor and process until minced. Add the apple and onion mixture to the food processor together with the breadcrumbs, mace, egg, sage leaves and a seasoning of salt and freshly ground black pepper. Process until evenly blended.
- Spoon the pork mixture into a large piping bag without a nozzle. Tie a knot at one end of each piece of sausage skin, then pipe in the mixture, leaving a 7.5cm (3in) gap to allow for shrinkage. Tie a knot at the other end of the skin. Chill the sausages for 30 minutes.
- Blanch the sausages in a pan of boiling water for 3 minutes. Drain and pat dry on kitchen paper.
- Heat the remaining oil in a large frying pan, add the sausages and cook for 5–8 minutes until golden all over. Serve with more salt and freshly ground black pepper.

Fagioli Borlotti, Spinaci e Aglio
Italian bean, spinach and garlic sausages

This is a great vegetarian sausage and could be served with wet polenta (see page 217) for a complete meal.

Makes 16 sausages
Preparation time: 20 minutes plus soaking overnight and chilling
Cooking time: about 1 hour 45 minutes

275g (10oz) dried borlotti beans, soaked overnight
8 garlic cloves, peeled
90ml (6 tablespoons) olive oil
3 onions, peeled and roughly chopped
450g (1lb) spinach, washed, tough stalks removed and patted dry
5ml (1 teaspoon) fresh thyme leaves, chopped
pinch of ground mace
pinch of freshly grated nutmeg
salt and freshly ground black pepper
1 egg, beaten
4m (4⅓yd) natural sausage skins, soaked, rinsed in cold water and cut into 25cm (10in) lengths

- Drain the beans and place in a large pan. Cover with fresh cold water. Bring to the boil, then cook for 1½ hours until quite tender. Drain. Place the beans in a food processor and process to a coarse purée. Leave until cold.
- Meanwhile, place the garlic cloves in a pan of cold water and bring to the boil. Drain and refresh in cold water, then finely chop.
- Heat 45ml (3 tablespoons) of the oil in a large frying pan, add the onions and chopped garlic and sauté for 5–8 minutes until soft. Stir in the spinach and cook for 3–5 minutes until wilted. Season with the thyme, mace, nutmeg and salt and freshly ground black pepper to taste. Transfer to the food processor and process until finely chopped. Cool.
- Mix the cooled spinach mixture with the beans and the egg.
- Spoon the sausage mixture into a piping bag without a nozzle. Tie a knot at one end of each piece of sausage skin, then pipe in the mixture, leaving a 7.5cm (3in) gap to allow for shrinkage. Tie a knot at the other end of the skin. Chill the sausages for 30 minutes.
- Blanch the sausages in a pan of boiling water for 3 minutes. Drain and pat dry on kitchen paper.
- Heat the remaining oil in a large frying pan and cook the sausages for 5–8 minutes until golden brown all over. Serve with more salt and freshly ground black pepper.

Anatra all'Arancia
Duck and orange sausages

Duck with orange has been a favourite flavour combination of mine for many years. Serve these sausages with crusty bread and lots of caramelised onions (simply cooked slowly in butter with a little honey). Or cut the sausages into small pieces and serve as cocktail party nibbles.

Makes 16 sausages
Preparation time: 20 minutes plus chilling
Cooking time: 15 minutes

75ml (5 tablespoons) olive oil
2 onions, peeled and finely chopped
2 garlic cloves, peeled and finely chopped
1.1kg (2½lb) skinned duck meat, minced
100g (4oz) rindless pork back fat, minced
finely grated zest of 1½ oranges
100g (4oz) fresh white breadcrumbs
pinch of ground mace
2.5ml (½ teaspoon) fresh thyme leaves
salt and freshly ground black pepper
1 egg, beaten
4m (4⅓yd) natural sausage skin, soaked, rinsed in cold water and cut into 25cm (10in) lengths

- Heat 30ml (2 tablespoons) of the oil in a frying pan, add the onions and garlic and sauté for 5 minutes until soft. Allow to cool.
- Place the duck meat and pork fat in a large bowl and add the onion mixture, orange zest, breadcrumbs, mace, thyme and a seasoning of salt and freshly ground black pepper. Mix in the egg.
- Spoon the sausage mixture into a piping bag without a nozzle. Tie a knot at one end of each piece of sausage skin, then pipe in the mixture, leaving a 7.5cm (3in) gap to allow for shrinkage. Tie a knot at the other end of the skin. Chill the sausages for 30 minutes.
- Blanch the sausages in a pan of boiling water for 3 minutes. Drain and pat dry on kitchen paper.
- Heat the remaining oil in a large frying pan and cook the sausages for 5–8 minutes until golden brown all over. Serve with more salt and freshly ground black pepper.

Salsicce di Porcini
Wild mushroom and saffron rice sausages

There's now an amazing selection of different mushrooms available in supermarkets, which I'm very pleased about as mushrooms are one of my favourite ingredients. Use fresh wild mushrooms for a special occasion; for everyday meals substitute field or flat mushrooms.

Makes 16 sausages
Preparation time: 20 minutes
Cooking time: 30 minutes

90ml (6 tablespoons) olive oil
1 onion, peeled and finely chopped
275g (10oz) risotto rice
150ml (5fl oz) dry white wine
1.2 litres (2 pints) hot chicken stock
5ml (1 teaspoon) saffron threads, soaked in 30ml (2 tablespoons) chicken stock
2 garlic cloves, peeled and crushed
275g (10oz) fresh porcini, wiped clean and finely chopped
salt and freshly ground black pepper
100g (4oz) unsalted butter, diced
100g (4oz) Parmesan cheese, freshly grated
4m (4⅓yd) natural sausage skin, soaked, rinsed in cold water and cut into 25cm (10in) lengths

- In a large deep pan, heat 60ml (4 tablespoons) of the olive oil. Add the onion and sauté for 5 minutes until soft. Stir in the rice and cook for a few seconds, then add the wine. Cook for 5 minutes until absorbed, stirring constantly. Gradually add the stock, a ladleful at a time, stirring and adding more stock as each batch is absorbed. The total cooking time will be about 20 minutes, at the end of which the rice should be *al dente*. Add the saffron half way through.
- Meanwhile, heat the remaining oil in a large frying pan. Add the garlic and porcini and cook for 5–10 minutes until the porcini are quite dry (they will give off a lot of water as they cook).
- Season the rice to taste with salt and freshly ground black pepper. Away from the heat, stir in the butter and Parmesan cheese, then mix in the porcini.
- Spoon the rice mixture into a piping bag without a nozzle. Tie a knot at one end of each piece of sausage skin, then pipe in the mixture, leaving a 7.5cm (3in) gap to allow for shrinkage. Tie a knot at the other end of the skin.
- To cook, poach the sausages in a pan of simmering water or stock for 10–15 minutes. Drain and serve immediately.

Desserts

Mascarpone alla Pera
Poached pears with mascarpone and cinnamon

Italians are not great sweet lovers, and I have to say that I am typical in this way – as a child I enjoyed fresh fruit after lunch or dinner. However, I really do like this delicious pear dessert. Most good Italian delis and supermarkets will stock amaretti biscuits.

Serves 4
Preparation time: 15 minutes
Cooking time: 30 minutes

4 large, firm, yet ripe pears
300ml (10fl oz) dry white wine
300ml (10fl oz) water
100g (4oz) caster sugar
1 whole clove
½ cinnamon stick
100g (4oz) soft light brown sugar

For the filling
120ml (8 tablespoons) mascarpone cheese
30ml (2 tablespoons) caster sugar
2 drops of vanilla essence
2 amaretti biscuits, crushed

- Peel the pears, leaving the stalks intact. Halve them lengthways and gently scoop out the core with a small teaspoon. Place the pear halves in a saucepan and add the wine, water, caster sugar and spices. Cover with greaseproof paper (the paper should touch the fruit) to prevent the pears from discolouring. Gently bring to the boil, then reduce the heat and simmer for 20 minutes until tender. Allow the pears to cool in the syrup.
- Lift out the pears with a slotted spoon and set aside. Strain the syrup, discarding the spices. Pour the syrup into a clean pan and add the brown sugar. Heat gently to dissolve the sugar, then boil for 5–10 minutes until you have a caramel. Leave to cool slightly.
- Meanwhile, mix the mascarpone with the sugar and vanilla essence. Fill the cavities in the pears with the mascarpone mixture. Place 2 pear halves on each plate and spoon over the caramel. Sprinkle with the crushed amaretti biscuits and serve immediately.

Fichi al Forno
Honey roast figs with tangerines

This is a beautifully simple recipe. Another one of my favourite ways of eating figs is peeled and served with Parma ham. Very Italian!

Serves 4
Preparation time: 15 minutes
Cooking time: 15 minutes

8 ripe figs
60ml (4 tablespoons) water
120ml (8 tablespoons) honey
75g (3oz) caster sugar
juice of 2 oranges
2 tangerines, peeled and separated into segments

- Pre-heat the oven to 190°C, 375°F, Gas Mark 5. Place the figs on a baking tray and sprinkle over the water. Bake for 7 minutes.
- Remove the figs from the oven. Drizzle over half of the honey, then return to the oven to bake for a further 5 minutes.
- Meanwhile, place the remaining honey, the sugar and orange juice in a small pan and heat gently to dissolve the sugar. Bring to the boil and boil for 5 minutes until a thick syrup forms.
- Split each tangerine segment lengthways, cutting along the outside edge, and open out to butterfly. Add half of the butterflied tangerine segments to the syrup and simmer for 2 minutes.
- Cut the figs open lengthways, in quarters, and arrange on 4 serving dishes. Spoon over the tangerine sauce and add the remaining butterflied tangerine segments. Serve warm.

Tortine di Cioccolato
Baby chocolate tarts with vanilla sauce

A very impressive dessert, this is the one for all chocolate lovers. The vanilla sauce perfectly complements the richness of the tart. When I cooked this on the photo shoot for the book we had to rescue it from being eaten before the photograph was taken! Michelle Collins adores this dessert.

Makes 8
Preparation time: 20 minutes
Cooking time: 30 minutes

75g (3oz) good-quality plain chocolate
275g (10oz) ready-rolled puff pastry
3 eggs
150g (5oz) caster sugar
30ml (2 tablespoons) cocoa powder
50g (2oz) unsalted butter, melted
100ml (4fl oz) milk
50g (2oz) pine nuts, ground

For the vanilla sauce
300ml (10fl oz) milk
50g (2oz) caster sugar
3 egg yolks
4 drops of vanilla essence

- Pre-heat the oven to 160°C, 325°F, Gas Mark 3. Break the chocolate into a heatproof bowl set over a pan of simmering water and heat gently for 3–5 minutes until the chocolate melts. Remove the bowl from the pan and set aside.
- Open out the puff pastry and stamp out 6 x 10cm (4in) rounds using a fluted pastry cutter. Mark a smaller circle (approx 8cm/3½in) in the centre of each round. Prick the borders with a fork. Place on a baking tray and bake for 10 minutes until well risen.
- Meanwhile, place the eggs, sugar and cocoa in a large bowl and whisk until thick and creamy. Gradually add the melted butter and milk, followed by the cooled chocolate and ground pine nuts.
- Remove the pastries from the oven. Gently press in the centre of each round to create a case. Pour the chocolate mixture into the cases. Return to the oven and bake for 20 minutes until well risen and just set to the touch.
- Meanwhile, make the vanilla sauce. Whisk all the ingredients together in a heatproof bowl

set over a pan of simmering water. Cook, stirring constantly, until the custard is slighly thickened. Remove the bowl from the pan and allow the custard to cool slightly (or make the sauce ahead of time and allow it to cool completely before serving).

- Serve the vanilla sauce with the warm tarts.

Torta di Ricotta
Ricotta cheesecake

Ricotta, like mascarpone, is very versatile and good for both sweet and savoury dishes. This dessert is quick to make, with a short list of ingredients, yet the result is impressive.

Serves 6
Preparation time: 20 minutes plus chilling to set

450g (1lb) fresh ricotta cheese
200g (7oz) icing sugar, sifted
4 eggs, beaten
60ml (4 tablespoons) Amaretto liqueur
5ml (1 teaspoon) vanilla essence
450ml (15fl oz) double cream
25g (1oz) good-quality plain chocolate, grated

- Lightly grease a 20cm (8in) round loose-based cake tin. Line the bottom and sides with greased greaseproof paper.
- In a large bowl, beat or whisk the ricotta with the icing sugar, eggs, Amaretto and vanilla essence until smooth. Whip the cream in another large bowl until soft peaks form. Mix one-third of the cream into the ricotta mixture, then fold in the remaining cream using a large metal spoon.
- Spoon the ricotta mixture into the prepared cake tin and level the surface. Chill for at least 4 hours until set.
- Remove the cake from the tin and gently peel off the paper. Sprinkle the cake with the grated chocolate to serve.

Crostata di Mascarpone
Mascarpone and lime tarts

Limes are a good alternative to lemons as they are refreshing, with a clean sharp taste. These tarts are perfect to serve after roasts or heavy main courses. One of my regular customers, Rebecca Williams, is a big fan of this dish but still manages to stay slim!

Makes 6
Preparation time: 30 minutes
Cooking time: 20 minutes

For the pastry
175g (6oz) plain flour
50g (2oz) caster sugar
75g (3oz) soft butter
15ml (1 tablespoon) water
1 egg white, beaten

For the filling
175g (6oz) mascarpone cheese
75g (3oz) caster sugar
2–3 drops of vanilla essence
grated zest and juice of 5 limes
225ml (8fl oz) double cream, lightly whipped
4 egg whites, stiffly whisked
25g (1oz) good-quality plain chocolate, grated

- To make the pastry, place the flour and sugar in a large bowl and rub in the butter until the mixture resembles breadcrumbs. Add the water and mix to form a dough. Turn out on to a lightly floured surface and knead gently for 2 minutes until smooth. Wrap in greaseproof paper and chill for 20 minutes.
- Preheat the oven to 190°C, 375°F, Gas Mark 5. Roll out the pastry dough and use to line 6 x 10cm (4in) loose-based tartlet tins. Trim the edges. Prick the pastry cases all over with a fork, then line with greaseproof paper and fill with baking beans. Place the tartlet tins on 1 or 2 large baking sheets. Bake blind for 15 minutes, removing the beans and paper lining after 10 minutes.
- Brush the pastry cases with beaten egg white and return to the oven to bake for a further 5 minutes (this seals the pastry and keeps it crisp once the filling is added). Remove from the tins and allow to cool.
- Meanwhile, make the filling. Put the mascarpone in a large bowl and mix with the sugar,

vanilla essence and lime zest and juice. Using a large metal spoon, fold the cream into the mascarpone mixture followed by the egg whites.

- Spoon the filling into the pastry cases and level the surfaces. Sprinkle with the grated chocolate. Chill for 30 minutes to set, then serve.

Espresso Brûlée

Although this isn't the easiest of desserts to prepare, it is worth all the effort. It is a variation on the French favourite, crème brûlée, *and definitely one of my preferred desserts.*

Serves 4
Preparation time: 10 minutes plus chilling
Cooking time: 1 hour

500ml (17fl oz) double cream
75ml (5 tablespoons) extra strong black coffee
6 egg yolks
2–3 drops of vanilla essence
45ml (3 tablespoons) caster sugar
demerera sugar for sprinkling

- Pre-heat the oven to 160°C, 325°F, Gas Mark 3. Place the cream and coffee in a large bowl and beat in the egg yolks, vanilla essence and caster sugar. Pour into 4 x 10cm (4in) ramekin dishes.
- Place the ramekins in a roasting tin lined with newspaper. Pour enough hot water into the tin to come half-way up the sides of the ramekin dishes. Cook in the oven for 1 hour until just set. Allow to cool, then chill for at least 4 hours.
- Pre-heat the grill to hot. Sprinkle an even layer of demerara sugar about 2mm (scant ⅛in) thick over the custards. Place under the grill for 3–5 minutes until the sugar melts and caramelises. Leave to cool a little so the caramel sets before serving.

Stella ai Marroni
Star-shaped sugared chestnut, chocolate and coffee cake

This rich chocolate and chestnut cake is utterly irresistible to chocoholics. Sugared chestnuts, also known as marrons glacés, *are easily found in delis and large supermarkets. If you don't have a star-shaped tin, you can bake the cake in a 20cm (8in) round tin.*

Serves 8
Preparation time: 20 minutes
Cooking time: 30–35 minutes

275g (10oz) best-quality plain chocolate, broken into pieces
200g (7oz) unsalted butter, diced
90ml (6 tablespoons) strong black coffee
25g (1oz) cocoa powder
6 eggs, separated
275g (10oz) sweetened chestnut purée
12 sugared chestnuts (*marrons glacés*)
icing sugar for dusting

- Pre-heat the oven to 200°C, 400°F, Gas Mark 6. Lightly grease a star-shaped cake tin, measuring 20cm (8in) from one point to the other. Line the bottom with greaseproof paper. Place the chocolate in a heatproof bowl with the butter and coffee. Set over a pan of simmering water and heat just until melted, stirring occasionally.
- Place the cocoa powder, egg yolks and chestnut purée in a large bowl and beat until smooth. Stir in the chocolate mixture. In a separate bowl whisk the egg whites until stiff, then fold into the chestnut mixture using a large metal spoon. Spoon into the prepared tin and level the surface.
- Bake for 30–35 minutes until the cake is dark brown and firm to the touch. Allow to cool in the tin for 10 minutes, then turn out on to a wire rack and leave to cool completely. Decorate with the sugared chestnuts and dust with icing sugar to serve.

Polenta alla Pera
Sweet polenta with pears and almonds

Polenta works very well when adapted to a sweet preparation. I discovered this unusual dessert when visiting my favourite holiday destination, Florence. That beautiful city has the most wonderful food, so I always look forward to trying new and exciting dishes every time I'm there.

Serves 8
Preparation time: 20 minutes
Cooking time: 30 minutes

6 eggs, separated
175g (6oz) caster sugar
200ml (7fl oz) Greek yoghurt
grated zest and juice of 1 orange
90g (3½oz) polenta flour
175g (6oz) ground almonds
2 poached pears (see Mascarpone alla Pera, page 174), thinly sliced
45ml (3 tablespoons) clear honey

- Pre-heat the oven to 180°C, 350°F, Gas Mark 4. Lightly grease a 20cm (8in) round cake tin. Line the bottom with greased greaseproof paper.
- Place the egg yolks in a large bowl and add the sugar. Whisk until thick and creamy. Stir in the yoghurt and orange zest. Using a large metal spoon, fold in the polenta flour and ground almonds. Whisk the egg whites in a separate bowl until stiff peaks form, then fold into the polenta mixture. Spoon into the prepared cake tin.
- Bake the cake for 30 minutes until golden brown and firm to the touch. Allow to cool slightly in the tin, then turn out and place on a large plate.
- Arrange the sliced pears over the top of the cake. Place the honey and orange juice in a small saucepan and heat through, then pour over the warm cake. Allow to cool before serving.

Torta alle Prugne
Prune cake with Vin Santo

A delicious fruit cake, this is ideal for coffee mornings or afternoon tea. It is essential to marinate the fruits overnight in the Vin Santo to ensure that they absorb the flavour of the wine and become thoroughly rehydrated, thus making the cake moist.

Serves 10
Preparation time: 30 minutes plus soaking overnight
Cooking time: 4 hours 30 minutes

800g (1¾lb) prunes
50g (2oz) glacé cherries, rinsed
50g (2oz) candied peel, rinsed
300ml (10fl oz) Vin Santo
225g (8oz) plain flour
1.25ml (¼ teaspoon) freshly grated nutmeg
2.5ml (½ teaspoon) ground mixed spice
225g (8oz) unsalted butter, softened
225g (8oz) soft light brown sugar or caster sugar
4 large eggs, beaten
50g (2oz) ground almonds
grated zest of 1 orange
grated zest of 1 lemon

- Place the prunes, cherries and candied peel in a large bowl and stir in the Vin Santo. Cover and leave at room temperature overnight.
- Pre-heat the oven to 140°C, 275°F, Gas Mark 1. Grease the bottom and sides of a 25cm (10in) round cake tin.
- Sift the flour and spices on to a large plate. Place the butter and sugar in a large bowl and beat together until light and creamy. Gradually beat in the eggs, 15ml (1 tablespoon) at a time. Fold in the flour mixture. Drain the fruit and add the fruit to the cake mixture together with the ground almonds and orange and lemon zests. Spoon into the prepared tin and level the surface.
- Cover the cake with foil and lightly pierce the foil with a skewer in several places. Bake at the bottom of the oven for 4½ hours until the cake is firm to the touch. Cool on a wire rack.

Mousse al Mandarino
Mandarin mousse with caramelised kumquats

Once you've assembled all the ingredients, this is a quick and easy recipe to make. Excellent served with soft amaretti biscuits.

Serves 6
Preparation time: 25 minutes plus chilling
Cooking time: 5 minutes

50g (2oz) mandarin orange zest, finely shredded
5 gelatine leaves or 25ml (1½ tablespoons) powdered gelatine
325ml (11fl oz) mandarin orange juice
4 egg whites
175g (6oz) icing sugar, sifted, plus more for dredging
450ml (15fl oz) whipping cream, lightly whipped
8 kumquats, halved lengthways

- Blanch the shreds of mandarin zest in boiling water for 6 minutes, then drain and refresh in cold water. Set aside.
- Soak the gelatine leaves in a little cold water to soften, then drain. If using powdered gelatine, soften in 45–60ml (3–4 tablespoons) warm water.
- Pour one-third of the mandarin juice into a pan, add the gelatine and heat gently until the gelatine dissolves. Stir in the remaining mandarin juice and the zest and set aside.
- Put the egg whites in a large bowl, add half of the icing sugar and whisk until soft peaks form. Gradually whisk in the remaining sugar and continue whisking until stiff peaks form. Slowly pour the cold mandarin mixture over the egg whites, continuously folding in with a large metal spoon. Gently fold in the whipped cream.
- Spoon into a large serving bowl and chill for 2–3 hours until set.
- Pre-heat the grill to hot. Dredge the cut sides of the kumquats with icing sugar and grill until the sugar has caramelised. Leave to cool.
- Top the mousse with the caramelised kumquats to serve.

Christmas

When I was a child, Christmas day was always a big occasion, particularly as we had a priest in the family (my brother). Everybody was up early for breakfast, and then ready for church. My mother wanted us to have wonderful food on such a special day and wanted to be able to be with us in church too, so her day used to start extra early as she had 9 of us to feed. The food really was worth all the effort, and we always appreciated it.

Modern families are much smaller, and generally people spend a lot less time cooking – one of the reasons for this being that you can now get a lot of things already prepared. But I think that it is important to make an effort on Christmas day, and involve the whole family in the preparation of the food. An excellent way to do this is to make fresh pasta, gnocchi or a big lasagne, with a good sauce such as fresh tomato or Bolognese. This will take several hours, so make the sauce a day before – the flavours can then mellow and improve. When you sit down to enjoy the finished dish, you will realise that it was time well spent.

Antipasti Misti
Mixed Italian hors d'oeuvres

There's not much cooking for you to do here, just assembling. I would recommend visiting an Italian deli for all the meats, to ensure that they are fresh and very thinly sliced. They will also be able to supply you with a good selection of marinated vegetables.

Serves 8
Preparation time: 20 minutes
Cooking time: 10 minutes

4 fresh Italian pork and fennel sausages
60ml (4 tablespoons) olive oil
1 x 400g (14oz) can cannellini beans, drained and rinsed
45ml (3 tablespoons) chopped fresh flat-leaf parsley
1 small red onion, peeled and finely chopped
salt and freshly ground black pepper
400g (14oz) mixed Italian meats, such as Parma ham, bresaola, salami, coppa and mortadella
400g (14oz) mixed marinated vegetables, such as oyster mushrooms, artichokes, courgettes, peppers and aubergines
1 jar mixed, herbed olives
sprigs of fresh flat-leaf parsley, to garnish

- Blanch the sausages in a pan of boiling water for 3 minutes. Drain. Heat a griddle until smoking, then add a little of the olive oil. Cook the sausages for 5–8 minutes until golden brown all over. Remove and cut diagonally into slices.
- Place the beans in a bowl and mix with the chopped parsley and red onion. Season well with salt and freshly ground black pepper. Drizzle on three-quarters of the remaining olive oil and mix well.
- Arrange the meats, marinated vegetables, bean salad, sausages and olives on a large platter or 8 small serving plates. Garnish with parsley sprigs and drizzle with the remaining olive oil to serve.

Lasagnetta Vegetariana
Mushroom and spinach lasagne

A good alternative for people who don't eat meat. It's also popular with children (my daughter Laura loves it and enjoys helping prepare it). I got this recipe from my wife Jan who regularly makes this for friends and family.

Serves 8
Preparation time: 30 minutes
Cooking time: 40–50 minutes

60ml (4 tablespoons) olive oil
1 large red onion, peeled and sliced
1 garlic clove, peeled and chopped
900g (2lb) mixed mushrooms, wiped clean and sliced
salt and freshly ground black pepper
2–3 sprigs of fresh tarragon, roughly chopped
20 sheets of fresh lasagne
1 quantity Salsa agli Spinaci (see page 205)
1 quantity Salsa al Pomodoro (see page 203)
1 quantity Salsa Besciamella (see page 206)
100g (4oz) Parmesan cheese, freshly grated

- Pre-heat the oven to 190°C, 375°F, Gas Mark 5. Heat the oil in a large pan, add the onion and garlic and fry for 5 minutes until soft. Stir in the mushrooms and sauté for 5 minutes. Season well with salt and freshly ground black pepper and add the tarragon. Set aside.
- Blanch the sheets of lasagne in a pan of boiling water until soft and pliable, then remove with a fish slice and plunge into a bowl of cold water. Drain and pat dry on kitchen paper.
- Line the bottom of a deep ovenproof dish with a layer of lasagne. Spoon over half of the mushroom mixture, then cover with layers of one-third of each of the sauces. Sprinkle with some Parmesan cheese. Repeat the layers, finishing with béchamel sauce and a sprinkling of Parmesan cheese.
- Bake for 30–40 minutes until golden brown and bubbling. Allow to stand for 10 minutes before serving.

Sorbetto al Limone
Lemon sorbet with prosecco

If serving more than three courses, it's good to have a sorbet half-way through the meal to refresh the palate. Prosecco is a popular Italian sparkling wine, a good alternative to champagne. It gives a great sense of festivity to pour the wine over the sorbet when serving.

Serves 8
Preparation time: 20 minutes plus freezing
*Cooking time:*10 minutes

175g (6oz) caster sugar
300ml (10fl oz) water
1 cinnamon stick
finely grated zest of 3 lemons
juice of 4 lemons
chilled prosecco wine, to serve

- Place the sugar, water and cinnamon stick in a pan and heat for 5 minutes until the sugar dissolves. Bring to the boil and boil for 10 minutes until a syrup forms. Discard the cinnamon stick and add the lemon zest and juice. Simmer for a further 2–3 minutes.
- Cool the lemon mixture, then pour into a freezerproof plastic container. Freeze for 2–3 hours until set. (Or use an ice cream machine, following the manufacturer's instructions.)
- To serve, scoop the sorbet into small serving glasses and pour over the prosecco wine.

Maiale Castagnolo
Roast loin of pork with chestnuts

Whole suckling pig is traditionally served at Christmas in Abruzzo, and this is an adaptation of that dish, using pork which is far more approachable. A pork roast may seem unusual, but this, along with ham, was the traditional English Christmas meat before turkey was introduced 40 or so years ago.

Serves 8
Preparation time: 1 hour
Cooking time: 2 hours

1 x 900g (2lb) boned loin of pork with crackling
2 sprigs of fresh rosemary, tough stalk discarded and leaves chopped
2 garlic cloves, peeled and chopped
10 fresh sage leaves
flaked sea salt
salt and freshly ground black pepper
roast potatoes, carrots and Brussels sprouts, to serve (see below)

For the stuffing
45ml (3 tablespoons) olive oil
1 medium onion, peeled and finely chopped
2 garlic cloves, peeled and chopped
10 fresh sage leaves, finely chopped
2 sprigs of fresh rosemary, tough stalks discarded and leaves finely chopped
10 no-soak dried apricots, finely chopped
100g (4oz) dried breadcrumbs
225g (8oz) canned chestnuts, drained
1 egg, beaten

For the gravy
60ml (4 tablespoons) Marsala wine
15ml (1 tablespoon) plain flour
450ml (15fl oz) meat stock

- Pre-heat the oven to 190°C, 375°F, Gas Mark 5. Remove the crackling (skin) from the loin of pork and score it. Mix the rosemary and garlic and rub over the pork loin. Place the sage leaves over the top, then place the cracking on the leaves. Tie with butcher's string to secure. If you have the bones from the pork, place them on the bottom of the roasting tin and sit the pork joint on top. Sprinkle with salt flakes. Roast for 2 hours.

- Meanwhile, make the stuffing. Heat the oil in a large frying pan, add the onion and garlic and cook for 5 minutes until soft. Away from the heat, stir in the herbs, apricots and breadcrumbs. Season well with salt and freshly ground black pepper. Chop half of the chestnuts and stir into the breadcrumb mixture. Mix in the egg. Roll the stuffing mixture into balls.
- Place the stuffing balls on a baking tray with the remaining whole chestnuts. Put into the oven to bake 10 minutes before the pork has finished roasting.
- Remove the pork from the oven (leave the stuffing balls and chestnuts in the oven to keep warm). Transfer the pork to a carving board and allow to rest in a warm place for 10 minutes.
- Remove as much of the fat as possible from the juices in the roasting tin, then place the tin on the hob. Add the Marsala wine and heat, stirring well to deglaze. Sprinkle over the flour and cook for 1 minute, then mix in the stock. Simmer for 5 minutes, stirring frequently. Season with salt and freshly ground black pepper.
- Slice the pork and arrange on a warmed platter. Place the stuffing balls and baked chestnuts around the pork and serve with the vegetables and gravy.

Roast potatoes: Allow 1 large baking potato per person, and peel and quarter lengthways. Blanch the potatoes in boiling salted water for 3 minutes, then drain. Arrange around the pork in the roasting tin, turn them over to coat with fat on all sides and roast for the final 30 minutes of the pork's cooking time.

Carrots and Brussels sprouts: Top and tail 450g (1lb) parisienne carrots (the little round ones), then cut them in half lengthways. Cook in a pan of boiling water for 10 minutes. Add 450g (1lb) trimmed Brussels sprouts to the pan and cook for a further 5 minutes. Drain. Melt 100g (4oz) butter in a large frying pan and stir in 50g (2oz) caster sugar until dissolved. Add the vegetables and cook for 3 minutes, stirring, until glazed.

Cavolo Rosso all'Agrodolce
Sweet and sour red cabbage with apples

You could use other cabbages in this recipe, such as 'black' cabbage, cavolo nero, or green cabbage, depending on the time of year, although red cabbage gives a wonderful rich colour. It's a great accompaniment to game dishes and sausages as well as pork.

Serves 4
Preparation time: 10 minutes plus marinating
Cooking time: 1 hour 30 minutes

1 small red cabbage
1 large cooking apple, peeled, cored and thickly sliced
juice of ½ lemon
1 onion, peeled and cut into wedges
50g (2oz) soft brown sugar
90ml (6 tablespoons) red wine vinegar
15ml (1 tablespoon) balsamic vinegar
1 bay leaf
25g (1oz) butter
salt and freshly ground black pepper

- Quarter the cabbage and cut out the core. Cut each quarter crossways into thin slices. Place in a large bowl. Toss the apple with the lemon juice, then add to the cabbage together with the onion, sugar, vinegars and bay leaf. Mix well. Cover and leave to stand for 2 hours.
- Pre-heat the oven to 160°C, 325°F, Gas Mark 3. Transfer the cabbage mixture to a casserole dish, dot with the butter and season with salt and freshly ground black pepper. Cover with a tight fitting lid and bake for 1½ hours until the cabbage is very soft. Adjust seasoning if necessary and serve.

Panettone ai Mirtilli
Panettone with cream and cranberries

This has to be the easiest and most delicious dessert for your Christmas lunch or dinner – simply heat the panettone, *make the cranberry sauce and finish off with cream. The dessert looks stunning and will give an Italian twist to your traditional English Christmas meal. You can buy* panettone *from all good Italian delis and some supermarkets.*

Serves 8
Preparation time: 15 minutes
Cooking time: 15 minutes

250g (9oz) fresh cranberries
100g (4oz) caster sugar
125ml (4fl oz) Vin Santo or dessert wine
4 amaretti biscuits, crushed
8 small *panettone*
50g (2oz) butter, cut into 8 knobs
300ml (10fl oz) double cream
25g (1oz) icing sugar, plus more for dusting

- Pre-heat the oven to 200°C, 400°F, Gas Mark 6. Place the cranberries in a pan with the caster sugar and Vin Santo. Simmer for 15 minutes until the cranberries are tender. Stir the amaretti biscuits into the cranberries.
- While the cranberries are cooking, quarter all the *panettone*, cutting down from the top but not all the way through the base. Put a knob of butter into each *panettone* and close up again. Place on a large baking tray and bake for 3–5 minutes.
- Pour the cream into a large bowl, add the icing sugar and whip until soft peaks form.
- Serve all the components for the dessert in separate large serving bowls, for your guests to assemble themselves. The *panettone* should be opened up and filled with cream and then topped with cranberry sauce. Sprinkle with icing sugar as the final touch.

Carnevale

In Italy, we say '*Carnevale ogni scherzo vale*', or 'Anything goes!' because this feast, which occurs the day before Ash Wednesday, marks the end of indulgence, before the restrictions of Lent begin.

Carnevale is quite a big occasion everywhere in Italy, but most especially in Venice and Viareggio. People from all over the world go there at this time of year. And it is no wonder – the bright colours of the costumes and the splendour of the procession, whether in the canals or streets, are truly spectacular. Masks are traditionally worn for *Carnevale*, and one Venetian mask, called a *bautta*, is particularly famous because you are able to eat and drink while wearing it and still remain anonymous.

As children, my brothers, sister and I would create our own fancy dress outfits by borrowing our parents' clothes and making masks at school. Once we had our costumes on, we would make our way into the village square, ready to take part in the big festival called *La Fagiolata*. For *Carnevale*, *Frittelle alle mele*, which are delicious deep-fried sweet pastries (see recipe on page 199) were made in all the local households and offered to anyone wearing a mask who knocked on the door.

Sformatini di Zucchini
Courgette and bacon tarts

Ideally serve this starter as soon as its cooked. For vegetarians, just skip the bacon to make delicious courgette tarts. These are also good for cocktail parties or small gatherings – always a great success in my house.

Makes 8
Preparation time: 25 minutes
Cooking time: 15–20 minutes

700g (1½lb) courgettes, trimmed
salt and freshly ground black pepper
4 rashers of smoked bacon, rind removed
50ml (2fl oz) olive oil
45ml (3 tablespoons) single cream
2 eggs, beaten
50g (2oz) plain flour
50g (2oz) Parmesan cheese, freshly grated

- Cut 3 of the courgettes into long, thin slices. Place in a colander, sprinkle with a little salt and leave to drain for 15 minutes.
- Meanwhile, grate the remaining courgettes on the coarse holes of a grater. Place in another colander, sprinkle with a little salt and leave to drain for 10 minutes.
- Using the blunt side of a knife, scrape along each rasher of bacon to stretch it until it is almost double in length. Cut across in half. Rinse the courgette slices and pat dry on kitchen paper.
- Pre-heat the oven to 190°C, 375°F, Gas Mark 5. Heat a griddle until almost smoking, then add a little of the oil and heat until hot. Lay the bacon and courgette slices on the griddle and cook for 2–3 minutes on each side until golden brown.
- Place 8 x 7.5cm (3in) metal flan rings on a large baking tray. Use the bacon and sliced courgettes to line the bottom and sides of each ring. Reserve some of the courgette slices for garnish.
- Rinse the grated courgettes, drain and pat dry on kitchen paper. Put in a bowl and beat in the cream, eggs, flour, Parmesan cheese and a seasoning of salt and freshly ground black pepper. Spoon the mixture into the lined rings, piling up into a mound in the centre.
- Bake the timbales for 15–20 minutes until the filling is just set and golden brown. Don't worry if a little of the egg mixture leaks out. Carefully lift off the rings and transfer the timbales to warmed serving plates. Garnish with the reserved courgette slices and serve immediately, drizzled with the remaining olive oil.

Gnocchi alla Romana
Semolina gnocchi gratin

You can make this gratin using mozzarella instead of Parmesan (or, even better, smoked mozzarella) and add some chopped mushrooms (sprinkle them over the gnocchi rounds before dotting with butter and grated cheese). Gnocchi has been a classic dish in Italian restaurants in England for some time, and it is good to see that it is now available ready-made in supermarkets. You can certainly use ready-made gnocchi in this recipe, making it very quick, and perfect for unexpected guests.

Serves 8
Preparation time: 15 minutes plus cooling and setting
Cooking time: 35 minutes

1 litre (1¾ pints) milk
5ml (1 teaspoon) salt
175g (6oz) semolina
100g (4oz) Parmesan cheese, freshly grated
1 egg
100g (4oz) butter, softened

- Place the milk and salt in a large pan and bring to just below boiling point. Gradually add the semolina, stirring constantly with a whisk to prevent any lumps from forming. Simmer for 15 minutes, stirring occasionally, until very thick. Remove from the heat and beat in 50g (2oz) of the Parmesan cheese and the egg.
- Wet a large work surface and spread the semolina mixture on it, in a layer about 1.5cm (½in) thick. Leave to cool and set.
- Pre-heat the oven to 190°C, 375°F, Gas Mark 5. Using a glass about 5cm (2in) in diameter, stamp out rounds from the set semolina mixture.
- Spread some of the butter over the bottom of a roasting tin or ovenproof serving dish. Layer the gnocchi rounds in the tin or dish, slightly overlapping them. Dot the layers with butter and sprinkle on some of the remaining cheese. Finish off with a sprinkling of cheese. Bake for 20 minutes until heated through and the cheese is melted and golden brown. Serve immediately.

Fegato alla Veneziana e Fichi
Calves' liver with onions, figs and red wine

This dish originates from Venice. Here is my version, which is my favourite way of cooking liver as it has lovely flavours. Take care not to overcook the liver – it should still be quite pink in the centre – otherwise it can tend to be quite dry. Chicken livers are delicious prepared in the same way.

Serves 8
Preparation time: 20 minutes
Cooking time: 20 minutes

30ml (2 tablespoons) olive oil
50g (2oz) butter
2 onions, peeled and cut into wedges
25g (1oz) plain flour
flaked sea salt and freshly ground black pepper
900g (2lb) calves' liver, thinly sliced
225g (8oz) seedless white grapes
4 purple figs, sliced into rounds
60ml (4 tablespoons) chopped fresh flat-leaf parsley
125ml (4fl oz) red wine
60ml (4 tablespoons) meat stock
Puré di Patate e Pastinaca, to serve (see below)
sprigs of fresh flat-leaf parsley, to garnish

- Heat the oil and half of the butter in a frying pan. Add the onions and stir well, then cook for 10 minutes until the onions are soft and beginning to caramelise.
- Meanwhile, place the flour on a plate and season with the salt and freshly ground black pepper. Add the liver to the flour and toss to coat both sides.
- Add the remaining butter to the frying pan, then put in the floured slices of liver and fry for 3–4 minutes until browned on both sides.
- Add the grapes, figs and chopped parsley and cook for 2 minutes. Stir in the wine and meat stock and simmer, stirring, for 5 minutes until the juices thicken. Serve immediately with the parsnip and potato purée, garnished with sprigs of parsley.

Puré di Patate e Pastinaca (Potato and parsnip purée): Peel and roughly chop 450g (1lb) each potatoes and parsnips. Put them in a large pan, cover with cold water and bring to the boil. Boil for 15–20 minutes until very tender. Drain and return to the pan. Mash with 60ml (4 tablespoons) crème fraîche, 25g (1oz) butter and a little milk. Season well with salt and freshly ground black pepper. Serve hot.

Frittelle alle Mele
Deep-fried pastry twists with caramelised apple

Traditionally these pastries – an Italian version of the doughnut – are eaten whilst chatting in the street with neighbours or given to children in their fancy dress when they knock on the doors. The pastries don't take long to make, so are good for parties.

Serves 8
Preparation time: 30 minutes
Cooking time: 20–25 minutes

For the apple sauce
350g (12oz) cooking apples, peeled, cored and chopped
50g (2oz) butter
50g (2oz) caster sugar
5ml (1 teaspoon) lemon juice
60ml (4 tablespoons) water

For the pastry twists
250g (9oz) plain flour
60ml (4 tablespoons) caster sugar
5ml (1 teaspoon) baking powder
pinch of salt
2 eggs, beaten
45ml (3 tablespoons) rum
vegetable oil for deep-frying
icing sugar for dusting (optional)

To serve
2 cooking apples, peeled, cored and thinly sliced into rings
60ml (4 tablespoons) demerara sugar

- For the sauce, place the apples in a saucepan with the butter, sugar, lemon juice and water. Cover with a damp piece of greaseproof paper (the paper should touch the fruit) and put on the lid. Cook over a very low heat for 15 minutes. The apples should be very tender but not browned. Mash the apples to a purée with a fork. Set aside to cool.
- Meanwhile, make the pastry twists. Sift the flour, sugar, baking powder and salt into a large bowl and make a well in the centre. Beat the eggs with the rum and pour into the well. Gradually beat in the flour mixture to form a rough dough. Turn the dough out on to a well-floured surface and knead until smooth.

- Divide the dough into quarters. Using one quarter at a time (and keeping the remainder well covered), roll out thinly and cut into 15cm (6in) long strips that are at least 2.5cm (1in) wide. Tie each strip into a knot. Repeat with the remaining dough.
- Heat enough oil in a large pan for deep-frying to 160–180°C, 325–350°F (a piece of dough dropped into the oil will sizzle and brown in 1 minute). Deep-fry the pastry twists, in batches of 4–6, for 1–2 minutes on each side. Drain on kitchen paper and allow to cool for 5 minutes, then dust with icing sugar if liked.
- Pre-heat the grill until hot. Place the apple rings on a foil-lined grill pan and sprinkle with half of the demerara sugar. Grill until the sugar caramelises. Turn the apples over, sprinkle with the remaining sugar and grill until golden brown and caramelised.
- Serve the pastry twists with the caramelised apples and apple sauce in a small separate bowl as a dip.

Basics

Salsa al Pomodoro
Traditional tomato sauce

A good home-made tomato sauce is a great base for many other sauces as well as delicious served by itself with pasta, meat or fish.

Serves 4
Preparation time: 10 minutes
Cooking time: 35 minutes

60ml (4 tablespoons) olive oil
1 small onion, peeled and finely chopped
1 garlic clove, peeled and crushed
1 x 800g (1¾lb) can chopped tomatoes
1 sprig of fresh rosemary, tough stalk discarded and leaves finely chopped
2 bay leaves
salt and freshly ground black pepper

- Heat the oil in a large deep pan, add the onion and cook over a very low heat for 5 minutes until soft but not browned.
- Stir in the garlic, tomatoes and rosemary. Add the bay leaves. Cook over a low heat for 30 minutes until the sauce is very thick.
- Season well with salt and freshly ground black pepper.

Ragù alla Bolognese
Bolognese sauce

This is a traditional recipe from Bologna. For a slight variation you can add chopped mushrooms or spinach; for a more delicate taste, stir in a little cream right at the end of cooking. If you prefer, use a mixture of beef and pork, or all pork.

Serves 4
Preparation time: 10 minutes
Cooking time: 1 hour 20 minutes

30ml (2 tablespoons) olive oil
40g (1½oz) butter
1 onion, peeled and finely chopped
1 celery stick, trimmed and finely chopped
1 carrot, peeled and finely diced
250g (9oz) lean mince (lamb, pork or beef)
200ml (7fl oz) red wine
250g (9oz) canned chopped tomatoes
salt and freshly ground black pepper

- Heat the oil and butter in a large deep pan, add the onion, celery and carrot and stir well. Cook over a gentle heat for 5 minutes until just beginning to soften.
- Add the mince and cook for 10 minutes, stirring frequently to break up any lumps. Add the red wine and simmer for 3 minutes. Stir in the tomatoes and season well with salt and freshly ground black pepper. Cook over a very low heat for 1 hour until the meat and vegetables are very tender. Stir occasionally during cooking.

Salsa agli Spinaci
Spinach sauce

This green sauce is good with poached eggs and pasta.

Serves 4
Preparation time: 10 minutes
Cooking time: 15 minutes

1kg (2¼lb) spinach, fresh or frozen chopped
50g (2oz) butter
225ml (8fl oz) milk
15ml (1 tablespoon) plain flour
salt and freshly ground black pepper

- If using fresh spinach, wash it and remove any tough stalks, then place the leaves in a large pan. Cover and cook over a low heat for 5 minutes until the leaves wilt. Drain well. Place in a food processor with the butter and milk and process until smooth. Transfer to a saucepan.
- If using frozen spinach, simply place it in a saucepan with the butter and milk and thaw over a low heat.
- Add the flour to the spinach mixture. Cook for 10 minutes, stirring occasionally. Season well with salt and freshly ground black pepper.

Salsa Besciamella
Béchamel sauce

This indispensable sauce can be used hot or cold. It can also be frozen.

Serves 4
Preparation time: 10 minutes
Cooking time: 15 minutes

450ml (15fl oz) milk
2 bay leaves
5ml (1 teaspoon) freshly grated nutmeg
40g (1½oz) butter
40g (1½oz) plain flour
salt and freshly ground black pepper

- Place the milk in a saucepan with the bay leaves and bring to just below boiling point. Remove from the heat and discard the bay leaves. Stir in the grated nutmeg
- In a separate pan, melt the butter and then stir in the flour. Cook for 1–2 minutes, stirring constantly, until a roux is formed. Away from the heat, gradually stir in the warm milk.
- Return the sauce to the heat and and cook over a gentle heat for 3–4 minutes, stirring constantly, until thickened. Season to taste with salt and freshly ground black pepper.

Bagna Cauda
Piemontese garlic and anchovy sauce

Serve this with plain roasted or boiled vegetables, which you dip into the hot sauce. In my opinion, Bagna Cauda is best served with cardoons, a vegetable that belongs to the artichoke family. Ensure that you wash the cardoons well, then peel and slice. Sprinkle the cardoons with lemon juice and water to prevent discoloration.

Serves 4
Preparation time: 5 minutes plus 2 hours soaking
Cooking time: 10 minutes

4 large garlic cloves, peeled and chopped
200ml (7fl oz) milk
100g (4oz) canned anchovy fillets, drained
225ml (8fl oz) olive oil
50g (2oz) butter

- Place the garlic in the milk and leave to soak for 2 hours.
- Remove the garlic with a slotted spoon and set aside. Add the anchovies to the milk and stir for a few minutes (this removes excess salt from the anchovies), then drain, discarding the milk.
- Place the oil and butter in a pan and add the anchovies and garlic. Cook over a low heat for 10 minutes until the anchovies are melted. It is important not to boil this sauce. A little cream can be added right at the end, if liked. Serve hot.

Pesto
Pesto sauce

Pesto can be red or green, depending on the basil available. Jars of pesto are now sold in every supermarket – these are all right in an emergency, but truly cannot compare with home-made. Pesto is excellent with trenette or linguine pasta and gnocchi or in soup such as minestrone.

Serves 4
Preparation time: 10 minutes

25g (1oz) fresh basil leaves
30ml (2 tablespoons) pine nuts
2 garlic cloves, peeled and finely chopped
225ml (8fl oz) extra virgin olive oil
25g (1oz) Parmesan cheese, freshly grated
75g (3oz) pecorino cheese, freshly grated
salt and freshly ground black pepper

- If using a pestle and mortar, grind the basil leaves with the pine nuts and garlic until smooth. Add some of the olive oil and grind to mix. Continue to add the oil and then the cheeses, grinding between additions, until you have a smooth paste. Season to taste with salt and freshly ground black pepper.
- If you do not have a pestle and mortar, place all the ingredients in a food processor and blend until smooth.

Salsa di Noci
Walnut sauce

This is a great sauce with ravioli and other filled pasta. Simply pour it over the hot pasta and heat through for 2–3 minutes.

Serves 4
Preparation time: 5 minutes

12 shelled walnuts
6 sprigs of fresh marjoram, finely chopped
120ml (8 tablespoons) extra virgin olive oil
25g (1oz) butter, softened
1 small garlic clove, peeled and finely chopped
200ml (7fl oz) single cream
salt and freshly ground black pepper

- Place the walnuts in a food processor and blend until finely chopped. Transfer to a bowl and add the marjoram and olive oil.
- In a separate bowl beat together the butter and garlic, then gradually mix in the walnut mixture followed by the cream. Season to taste with salt and freshly ground black pepper.

Tapenade
Olive paste

Tapenade is excellent served simply spread on rustic Italian bread, or it can be mixed with freshly cooked pasta or vegetables such as fennel or cauliflower.

Serves 4
Preparation time: 5 minutes

100g (4oz) stoned black olives
1 garlic clove, peeled and chopped
25g (1oz) canned anchovy fillets, drained
15g (½oz) capers
squeeze of lemon juice
3 fresh basil leaves
15ml (1 tablespoon) olive oil
freshly ground black pepper

- Place the olives in a food processor with the garlic, anchovies, capers, lemon juice, basil leaves and olive oil. Season with plenty of freshly ground black pepper. Process until quite smooth.

Fish stock

If storing the stock, cool first and then chill or freeze in bags of 300ml (10fl oz) quantities.

Makes 1.2 litres (2 pints)
Preparation time: 10 minutes
Cooking time: 55 minutes

1kg (2¼lb) fish bones, from sole, monkfish or sea bream
2.4 litres (4 pints) water
100g (4oz) onions, peeled and chopped
100g (4oz) fennel, chopped
100g (4oz) celery, chopped
100g (4oz) carrots, peeled and chopped
100g (4oz) leeks, chopped
4 bay leaves

- Place the fish bones in a large pan with the water. Bring to the boil, skimming the surface of any scum. Simmer gently for 25 minutes. Strain through a sieve.
- Pour the strained liquid into a clean pan and add all the vegetables and bay leaves. Simmer for a further 30 minutes until the stock is reduced to 1.2 litres (2 pints). Strain again and discard the vegetables.

Vegetable stock

This stock will keep in the refrigerator for up to 3 days.

Makes 1.5 litres (2½ pints)
Preparation time: 20 minutes
Cooking time: 1 hour 15 minutes

60ml (4 tablespoons) olive oil
2 onions, peeled and chopped
2 garlic cloves, peeled and chopped
4 carrots, peeled and sliced
2 large leeks, trimmed and sliced
2 celery sticks, trimmed and chopped
2 large potatoes, peeled and chopped
150ml (5fl oz) dry white wine
4 ripe tomatoes, roughly chopped
1 bouquet garni
30ml (2 tablespoons) flaked sea salt
1.8 litres (3 pints) water

- Heat the oil in a large pan, add the onions and garlic and cook for 5 minutes until soft. Stir in the carrots, leeks, celery and potatoes. Cook for 10 minutes, stirring occasionally, until soft but not browned.
- Add the wine and boil for 5 minutes until the liquid is completely evaporated. Add the tomatoes, bouquet garni, salt flakes and water. Bring back to the boil, then reduce the heat. Partially cover the pan and leave to simmer for 1 hour.
- Strain the stock through a sieve into a bowl. If a concentrated stock with a stronger flavour is required, return the liquid to the pan and reduce further by boiling (without the vegetables). Use as required.

Chicken stock

For a clear stock, it is important not to boil the liquid with the flavourings. If you do end up with a cloudy stock, simply whisk some egg whites with a fork, add to the hot stock and heat for 2–3 minutes, then strain again. This stock is perfect for risottos.

Makes 1.8 litres (3 pints)
Preparation time: 20 minutes
Cooking time: 45 minutes

1 whole chicken or 450g (1lb) chicken legs or wings
30ml (2 tablespoons) olive oil
100g (4oz) carrots, peeled and chopped
2 celery sticks, trimmed and chopped
4 bay leaves
1 onion, peeled and halved
2.4 litres (4 pints) water

- Place all the ingredients in a large pan with the water. Bring to the boil, skimming the surface of any scum that rises to the surface. Reduce the heat and leave to simmer for 45 minutes.
- Strain through a sieve lined with muslin and allow to cool. Chill the stock in the refrigerator, then skim off any fat that has set on the surface.

Fresh pasta

Use free-range or organic eggs for the best flavour and colour.

Serves 8
Preparation time: 30 minutes plus standing

1kg (2¼lb) type 00 strong white pasta flour
10 eggs
2 egg yolks

- Sift the flour onto a large work surface and make a well in the centre. Crack the eggs into a large bowl, add the egg yolks and whisk together. Pour into the well in the flour.
- With clean fingertips, mix the flour into the eggs until a paste or wet dough is formed. Wash and dry your hands, then flour them.
- Knead the dough until it is smooth and springs back when pressed. Cover with cling film and leave to rest for 30 minutes (if making stuffed pasta, such as ravioli, use the dough immediately).
- Divide the dough into three or four portions. For tagliatelle or fettuccine, roll out each portion of dough on a well floured surface as thinly as possible and cut into long strips about 5mm (¼in) wide; for pappardelle, cut the strips twice as wide. (Or use a pasta machine for rolling and cutting.)
- Toss the strips with flour to prevent them from sticking together, and keep on a large plastic tray until required. (If not cooking the pasta straight away, freeze it.)
- To cook the pasta, add it to a very large pan of boiling salted water and cook until it rises to the top and is *al dente*.

Spinach pasta dough: Add 250g (9oz) well-drained spinach purée to the eggs before incorporating the flour.

Gnocchi di Patate
Basic potato gnocchi

The small dumplings called gnocchi can be made from potato, semolina or spinach and ricotta. The type of gnocchi and the way in which they are served varies from region to region – these potato gnocchi are typical of northern Italy. Gnocchi used to be served as a first course, but today it is more common to enjoy them as a main dish.

Serves 4
Preparation time: 30 minutes
Cooking time: 30 minutes

1kg (2¼lb) potatoes, scrubbed
300g (11oz) plain flour
1 egg
5ml (1 teaspoon) salt
25g (1oz) butter

To serve
Pesto (see page 208) or other sauce
freshly grated Parmesan cheese

- Place the unpeeled potatoes in a large pan and cover with water. Bring to the boil, then cook for 20 minutes. Drain and peel while still warm.
- Pass the potatoes through a mouli-légumes or sieve into a large bowl. Add half of the flour, the egg, salt and butter. Work together with your hands to make a homogenous dough, adding more of the flour if necessary. Turn out on to a surface sprinkled with the remaining flour and roll the dough into several ropes that are 2.5cm (1in) thick. Cut the ropes across into 2cm (¾in) pieces. Shape the gnocchi by rolling the pieces over the back of a fork. Spread out on a floured tea towel.
- Bring a large pan of salted water to the boil. Reduce to a simmer. Place the gnocchi in the pan, in batches, and cook for 2–3 minutes until they rise to the surface. Drain and keep warm while cooking the remaining gnocchi.
- Once all the gnocchi are cooked, toss in your favourite sauce and serve sprinkled with Parmesan cheese. My favourite sauces are pesto or fresh tomatoes and basil drizzled with extra virgin olive oil.

Focaccia

Probably the most popular Italian bread on the market at the moment. It's very easy to make your own, and the fresher it is, the better!

Serves 6
Preparation time: 20 minutes plus proving
Cooking time: 15 minutes

700g (1½lb) strong white bread flour
5ml (1 teaspoon) salt
20g (¾oz) easy-blend dried yeast
90ml (6 tablespoons) olive oil
450ml (15fl oz) lukewarm water
flaked sea salt
1 sprig of fresh rosemary, tough stalk discarded and leaves roughly chopped

- Sift the flour and salt into a large bowl and stir in the yeast. Rub in 60ml (4 tablespoons) of the olive oil until the mixture resembles fine breadcrumbs. Stir in the lukewarm water to form a rough dough.
- Turn out the dough onto a well-floured surface and knead until the dough is smooth and springs back when gently pressed. Place in a lightly oiled bowl and cover with cling film. Leave to rise in a warm place for 45 minutes until almost doubled in size.
- Pre-heat the oven to 220°C, 425°F, Gas Mark 7. Gently knead the dough to knock out the air, then roll out to a rectangle or square about 2cm (¾in) thick. Place on a large greased baking sheet.With floured fingers, make indentations at 2.5cm (1in) intervals all over the dough. Drizzle over the remaining oil and sprinkle over salt flakes and the rosemary.
- Bake the focaccia for 5 minutes, then reduce the oven to 200°C, 400°F, Gas Mark 6. Continue baking for 10 minutes until the bread is golden brown. Serve warm or cold.

Polenta

Polenta has become a fashionable addition to many menus in this country, but has been a staple of the diet in Italy for many years.

Serves 4
Preparation time: 5 minutes
Cooking time: 25 minutes

1.75–2 litres (3–3½ pints) water
5ml (1 teaspoon) salt
350g (12oz) polenta flour
125g (5oz) butter (optional)
200g (7oz) Parmesan cheese, freshly grated

- Place the water in a large deep pan, add the salt and bring to the boil. Reduce the heat and gradually add the polenta flour to the water, stirring constantly with a whisk. When the polenta is completely blended in, simmer for 20 minutes, stirring occasionally, until the polenta is very dense and thick and is coming away from the sides of the pan.
- For wet polenta, beat the butter and Parmesan cheese into the hot polenta and season with plenty of freshly ground black pepper. Serve immediately.
- For set polenta, omit the butter and beat the Parmesan cheese into the hot polenta. Spread the polenta in a large baking tray in a layer about 2.5cm (1in) thick. Leave to cool. Once the polenta has set, cut it into squares or other shapes. Brush with oil and toast under a pre-heated hot grill for 2 minutes on each side until golden brown and crisp.

Risotto

When making risotto, always use risotto rice, such as Arborio, which is available from all good supermarkets.

Serves 4
Preparation time: 20 minutes
Cooking time: 20–25 minutes

75g (3oz) butter
1 onion, peeled and finely chopped
350g (12oz) risotto rice
1.5 litres (2½ pints) hot vegetable stock
salt and freshly ground black pepper
100g (4oz) Parmesan cheese, freshly grated

- Melt 50g (2oz) of the butter in a deep pan, add the onion and sauté for 5–8 minutes until soft. Stir in the rice and stir for a few more seconds.
- Gradually add the stock, a ladleful at a time, stirring and adding more stock as each batch is absorbed. The total cooking time will be about 20 minutes, at the end of which the rice should be *al dente*. Season to taste with salt and freshly ground black pepper.
- Stir the remaining butter into the risotto together with three-quarters of the Parmesan cheese. Allow the risotto to rest for 2–3 minutes, then serve with the remaining Parmesan cheese and more freshly ground black pepper.

Glossary

Al dente: literally 'to the tooth', this term denotes pasta, rice or vegetables perfectly cooked until tender but still retaining some bite or firmness.

Beard: the silky filaments on mussel shells by which the mussels attach themselves to rocks. When cleaning mussels for cooking, scrape off any beards with a knife (farmed mussels do not have beards).

Blanch: to submerge food in boiling water for a brief period of time, to soften, whiten or remove excess saltiness. Tomatoes and some fruits are blanched to make the skins easy to peel off; root vegetables are blanched to remove excess starch.

Coulis: a purée of fruits or vegetables, served as a sauce.

Deglaze: to loosen browned sediment from the bottom of a frying pan or roasting tin after cooking, using liquid such as wine or stock and stirring and scraping well.

Flambé: to set wine or other spirit alight, to burn off alcohol and thereby mellow the flavour.

Frittata: a flat omelette with a firm texture.

Marinate: to soak meat, fish or vegetables in a seasoned liquid to tenderise and/or add flavour.

Ragù: the Italian word for a meat sauce or stew.

Reduce: to boil a liquid such as a stock or sauce to evaporate some of it, thereby intensifying the flavour.

Refresh: to rinse hot freshly cooked food, usually green vegetables, with very cold water, or iced water, to stop further cooking.

Risotto: a rice dish with a creamy consistency; usually savoury.

Roux: a cooked mixture of butter and flour used as the base for sauces.

Sauté: to pan fry quickly in a small quantity of fat, stirring and tossing the food constantly.

Sear: to brown the outside of meat very quickly, in a frying pan, under the grill or in the oven.

Sweat: to cook food, usually vegetables, gently in a small quantity of fat, covered with damp greaseproof paper and a lid, until soft but not browned.

Zest: coloured part of skin of citrus fruit.

Index

calves' liver with onions, figs and
red wine, 198
cannellini beans, 1
mixed Italian hors d'oeuvres,
188
three bean soup, 124
Tuscan white bean soup, 121
Cape Sante al Rosmarino, 16
capers, 2
sautéed broccoli with butter
and capers, 132
Caprino alla Pera, 47
Capriolo al Ginepro, 162
Capriolo all'Oliva, 156
Carnevale, 195-200
Carrè d'Agnello al Rosmarino,
97-8
carrots:
carrots and Brussels sprouts,
192
Gorgonzola, fennel and carrot
salad, 50
Cavolo Rosso all'Agrodolce,
193
Ceci e Patate, 117
celeriac:
roast fillet of hare with port
and redcurrant sauce, 154
Cervo al Finocchio Selvatico, 15
cheese, 5-6
artichoke, mozzarella and herb
risotto, 42
asparagus and mascarpone
risotto, 37
asparagus gratin with
Parmesan, 54
baby macaroni with traditional
Bolognese sauce, 245
baked sweet potatoes with
leeks and mozzarella, 55
buffalo mozzarella, wild baby
rocket and roasted pepper
salad, 44
deep-fried chicken breasts
stuffed with fontina and
ricotta cheeses, 78-9
deep-fried stuffed pizzas, 116
focaccia stuffed with

mozzarella and mortadella,
17
fresh salmon, spinach and
ricotta sausages, 169
fresh spinach with garlic, chilli
and Parmesan, 131
fried mozzarella with pizza
sauce, 114
Gorgonzola, fennel and carrot
salad, 50
Italian beef and pork burgers,
152
milk, Parmesan and rocket
risotto, 33
mini pizzas party-style, 115
mixed leaf and feta salad, 52
pan-fried pizza bread, 111
pesto sauce, 208
polenta with fresh tomato,
basil and ricotta, 138
pork chops stuffed with
smoked mozzarella and
sage, 70
pork fillet wrapped with
courgettes and melting
dolcelatte, 75
risotto, 218
roast vegetable and rigatoni
bake, 25
salad of poached pear with
grilled goat's cheese, 47
semolina gnocchi gratin, 197
smoked mozzarella wrapped in
Parma ham, with pear and
radicchio, 94
steamed escarole, porcini and
Parmesan salad, 45
stuffed chicken supremes with
Parma ham and Parmesan
cheese, 71
venison fillet with fennel and
Parmesan, 15
wild mushroom and barley
risotto in Parmesan baskets,
35-6
see also mascarpone
cheesecake, ricotta, 178
chestnuts:

roast loin of pork with
chestnuts, 191-2
star-shaped sugared chestnut,
chocolate and coffee cake,
182
chicken:
chicken breasts with pineapple
and bok choy, 77
chicken stock, 213
deep-fried chicken breasts
stuffed with fontina and
ricotta cheeses, 78-9
risotto with chicken, Parma
ham and brandy, 38
roasted spring chickens, 74
sliced chicken supremes with
sweet peppers, 80
stuffed chicken supremes with
Parma ham and Parmesan
cheese, 71
chickpeas, 1
chickpea and potato soup, 117
chicory, baby sweetcorn, radicchio
and red onion salad, 46
chillies, 6
fillet steak with garlic and chilli
sauce, 149-50
fresh spinach with garlic, chilli
and Parmesan, 131
chocolate:
baby chocolate tarts with
vanilla sauce, 176-7
pancake tagliolini with white
chocolate ice cream and
raspberry coulis, 84-5
star-shaped sugared chestnut,
chocolate and coffee cake,
182
vanilla mousse with dark
chocolate sauce, 82-3
Christmas, 187-94
clams:
cuttlefish and clam risotto, 32
fish soup Pescara-style, 57-8
linguine pasta with scallops,
clams and leeks, 23
seafood and wild mushroom
salad, 43